SETTLE IT YOURSELF

SETTLE IT YOURSELF
— WHO —
NEEDS A
LAWYER

DOROTHEA
KAPLAN J.D.

FRED
BENJAMIN J.D.

**A consumer's guide for
collecting
personal injury claims,
accident claims,
and property damage claims.**

Chicago

89   88   87   86   85   5   4   3   2   1

Library of Congress Catalog Card Number:
85-71295

International Standard Book Number:
0-933893-01-9

Bonus Books, Inc.
160 East Illinois Street
Chicago, Illinois 60611

Printed in the United States of America

Contents

List of Forms

Preface

Have you ever suffered an accidental injury and decided not to seek compensation because you weren't sure how to get started? Were you reluctant to bother a lawyer with what you thought was too small or too "iffy" a case? Or perhaps you were concerned about expensive legal fees. If so, this book's for you.

Remarkably, insurance industry studies show that people whose economic losses are more than $2,000 usually receive larger net settlements when they don't use a lawyer. And claimants in most instances receive their money five times faster from an insurance company when they do it themselves.

With *Settle It Yourself* you can easily and successfully process your accident claim straight through to a cash settlement with the insurance company. Simplified, step-by-step procedures help you recover compensation for bodily injury and property damage—without using a lawyer. An easy-to-follow format puts the know-how for collecting a cash settlement at your fingertips.

Even if you have never had an accidental injury, *Settle It Yourself* will leave you solidly prepared and confident should you ever be confronted with a personal injury or property damage claim situation.

It would be startling to know how many millions of dollars are left unclaimed each year simply because a few routine forms were never sent to the insurance comany. *Settle It Yourself* will help you keep your dollars from being part of those millions.

Acknowledgments

We appreciate the efforts of a number of people who helped us prepare this book. Among those who have our deepest thanks are Christine Adenau, Charlene Baaske, Joan Eagle, Kathleen Engel, Andrew Kagan, Carol Karton, Gary Katz and Sandra Pesmen.

Introduction

Welcome to the world of legal self-help. A place we hope will be comfortable and rewarding.

The world of legal self-help is new. As little as two to three years ago, the consumer would not have had access to the kind of legal information offered here. At that time, the only avenue open to a layperson who wanted to make an accidental injury claim was hiring a lawyer. Information giving people the ability to do this for themselves was unavailable in the legal service market place.

Recent sweeping changes have redefined what the public can expect of the legal profession. Lawyers too have been forced to rethink the nature of their obligations to the consumer.

The gap between the public's desire for legal services at an affordable rate and the lawyer's obligation to serve the public, not only as a hired advocate, but also in a way that meets the consumers needs, is beginning to close.

The know-how given here opens a new road for consumers, hands them additional power over their lives, and enables them to proceed in a formerly lawyer-dominated endeavor.

The consumer, however, is not the only beneficiary here. Unexpectedly, the authors too have gained. Laboring to express technical ideas, formerly presented to the public only in legalese, caused us to leave the cloistered world of the advocate and enter the riskier world of the communicator.

We began this endeavor as legal practitioners, believing that a few standard forms accompanied by short explanations would get our point across. Our work looked dreary. Next we became writers and began to weave many of our own thoughts and experiences into the text. The copy gained dimension. Finally, relying on the people we are, we reached down deep inside and added the qualities that give a work life—our judgment, our feelings, and our spirit. At last it was breathing.

Also, while writing, we remembered other legal self-help books we had read. Each, we recalled, was filled with a "cutesiness" that masked the legal revelations promised by the book's title. People can look to legal self-help as a viable resource, but only where actual self-help techniques are furnished by the authors. That is why our approach here is uncluttered and straightforward. No "Aunt Minnie" stories or pseudo-amusements, just procedures you can trust for what they can and will do for you.

The role of the lawyer as a communicator of legal information has begun. Not only does this role satisfy an intense consumer need, but it also confirms our own commitment to an honorable profession.

The How-To's, The What-To's and The Why-Don't-You's

This easy-to-use book is a complete guide for handling your own routine personal injury or property damage claims against an insurance company. All the information you'll need is here, as well as a set of ready-to-use forms. But, before moving ahead into the world of self-help, we'd like to answer some of your questions.

What kind of accident or personal injury can I collect for?

Everyday situations produce many kinds of accidental occurrences. Sometimes these come about when another person or business fails to use reasonable care for your safety. At other times, accidents happen to us just because we are in the wrong place at the wrong time. It's even possible that sometimes our property is damaged or harm is caused us by our own carelessness or inadvertance. These commonplace occurrences could produce accident claim situations. We'll show you how to collect for them — without a lawyer — and also let you know when it makes sense to use legal help.

- A driver runs through a stop sign, striking your car and knocking you against the windshield.

- A grocer leaves a slippery spill on the aisle floor, causing you to slip and fall.

- Your landlord allows torn carpeting to remain on a stairway, causing you to trip and fall down a flight of stairs.

- A construction company carelessly does sewer work outside your house, causing broken windows and foundation damage.

- A motel owner's security guards mistake you for someone else and beat you up while you're a guest in your room.

- An airline does not properly maintain its passenger stairs, causing you to fall down the stairs while exiting the plane.

- A department store's stock clerk, when pushing empty baskets down the store aisles, wheels them into you, knocking you to the ground.

- An uninsured driver strikes your auto in the rear while you are stopped at a red light, throwing you and your passenger into the dashboard and damaging your auto.

- While visiting in a friend's backyard, your child runs into a hot barbecue kettle and burns herself.

- While jogging on the street, you are struck by a car.

What kind of damages can I collect for?

Whenever an accident happens and you experience any of the kinds of damages listed here, you are entitled to be made whole again by the negligent person's insurance company, or your own insurance company — or perhaps both:

- Medical and hospital expenses.

- Medical and hospital expenses likely to be incurred in the future.

- Value of time, salaries, or earnings lost.

- Value of time, salaries, or earnings likely to be lost in the future.

- Cost of repair or the value of damaged property.

- Pain and suffering.

- Disfigurement.

- Disability.

- Aggravation of a pre-existing condition or ailment.

- Miscellaneous expenses such as household help during disability, broken eyeglasses, torn clothing, prescribed medications, or rental cost of substituted property.

When can I make a claim against another person's insurance company?

A claim for damage or injury stemming from a *motor vehicle* accident is made against the negligent driver's or owner's insurance company in a state that has a fault system of automobile insurance. (See Appendix A for a list of fault and no-fault states.)

Even in most states that have a no-fault system of automobile insurance, that part of your auto accident claim not covered by your own insurance company because of dollar-limit restrictions or the type of personal injury suffered, can be made against the negligent other driver's or owner's insurance company.

In all states, personal injury or property damage claims not related to the use of a motor vehicle are made against the negligent person's insurance company. Therefore, any claim against the grocer who leaves a slippery spill on the floor or the landlord who allows torn carpeting to remain in a building hallway, is made against the owner's insurance company.

Sometimes, medical payment claims are made against another person's insurance company. When you are a passenger injured in an auto accident or hurt while at someone else's home, the cost of any medical treatment is reimbursed without regard to fault by the driver's or homeowner's or tenant's insurance company. Reimbursement is limited to a dollar amount stated in the policy.

When can I make this claim against my own insurance company?

You can make a claim with your own liability insurer in any of the following situations.

In about one-half of the states, the laws require that your medical and hospital expenses and loss of earnings growing out of an auto accident, whether you are riding in a motor vehicle or are a pedestrian, be reimbursed without regard to fault by your own insurance company. This is known as a no-fault or personal injury protection (PIP) automobile insurance plan.

In all states, *medical expenses* incurred because of injuries suffered while using your auto will be reimbursed under your own auto liability policy. There is a set dollar amount per person per incident limit. Payment is made without regard to fault.

Claims for *collision damage, fire, or theft* of your insured motor vehicle — car, boat, van, truck, or motorcycle — are made under your own insurance policy without regard to fault, but subject to a deductible amount. Therefore, if your parked car is struck by an unknown driver, or your car is vandalized, or you run your boat into a buoy, it is your insurance company that gives you reimbursement over and above your deductible amount as long as you have purchased collision and/or comprehensive coverage.

Whenever the other negligent driver is an uninsured motorist or an unidentifiable hit-and-run driver, your damage or injury claim, whether living in a fault or a no-fault state, is made with your own insurance company. These uninsured motorist benefits can be claimed even when you are a pedestrian injured by an uninsured motorist or an unidentifiable hit-and-run driver.

If I hire a lawyer, how much will it cost?

Ordinarily, when a lawyer is hired to file accidental injury or property damage claims, the fee charged is one-third of all amounts recovered. When the claim cannot be settled and a lawsuit must be filed, the lawyer's share can go up as high as forty or fifty percent of your recovery. See chapter 5 for an in-depth look at cases where you probably should hire a lawyer.

How do I get the best results from this book?

Read the material carefully and follow the step-by-step procedures mapped out in the chapters that follow. A systematic and well-documented approach is the best way to make a successful claim. A few key recommendations also will help:

- Type correspondence whenever possible, always keeping a copy for yourself.
- Collect all documentation of damage and injury before submitting the claim for settlement. Don't submit the claim piecemeal.

- Save all original property damage repair estimates or paid bills, all witness statements, photographs, medical reports, hospital records, and medical and hospital bills.

- Read your auto liability and homeowner's or tenant's insurance policies so that you are familiar with the coverage and benefits you've purchased.

What if I can't make a settlement with the insurance company?

If the claim process with the negligent party's company or even your own company does not bear fruit or if the settlement offer is not acceptable to you, a lawyer can be consulted or perhaps hired to represent you. At this stage, however, an attorney acting as a consultant can be paid on an hourly basis. By having the insurance adjuster put his final offer in writing and by having ready access to all information supporting your claim, a lawyer can accurately evaluate your case. If you later decide to hire a lawyer, he may agree to charge a fee based on the amount recovered over and above the insurance company's top written offer to you.

Now get started and good luck!

The Jargon

You've probably heard most of these terms before and already are familiar with their meanings. Their use in this format, however, may differ from your customary understanding of them. Just so that there is no confusion, we've defined the words listed here, not in a technical way, but in a way that fits in with their use in this book.

The person employed by the insurance company who investigates and then negotiates your accident claim with you.

Claims Adjuster

Where the amount of your accidental injury and damage compensation is reduced by the percentage of negligence attributable to you.

Comparative Fault or Comparative Negligence

The money paid to you which includes not only your dollar for dollar injury expenses, but also an extra amount for the general or intangible damages you've suffered.

Compensation

Where you cannot recover *any* damages at all from the negligent party's insurance company because your own negligence helped to cause your accident or injury.

Contributory Negligence

The amount of money stated in your policy that the insurance company deducts before reimbursing you for each kind of claim made.

Deductible

Where responsibility to pay you for any damage or injury is born entirely by the negligent driver's or owner's liability insurer.

Fault Automobile Insurance

Immeasurable non-financial losses that are incurred when you have bodily injury, such as pain and suffering, disfigurement, disability, aggravation of a pre-existing condition, or permanency of an injury. Compensation is not measured for these in an exact way, but rather with the goal of making you whole again.

General or Intangible Damages

The dollar amount your insurance company is obligated to pay for personal injuries or property damage resulting from your negligence.

Liability Coverage

Medical Payment	Reimbursement given by your auto liability insurer to you as an injured driver, passenger, or pedestrian, or any injured passengers for medical and hospital expenses that resulted from an auto accident. Similar coverage is provided under your homeowners's or tenant's policy to any persons, except household members, injured in your home.
Negligence	Unintentional actions or inactions that are the underlying causes of an accident.
No-Fault Automobile Insurance	Where you, the insured, are reimbursed by your own auto insurance company without regard to fault for certain kinds of damages resulting from an automobile accident.
Personal or Bodily Injury	The physical, mental, or emotional harm caused by the accident.
Property Damage	The costs of repairing or replacing damaged personal property.
Reimbursement	Money paid which represents only dollar for dollar repayment of your damages or injury expenses.
Special Damages	The actual financial costs you've been subjected to because of the accident such as present and future medical and hospital expenses, present and future lost earnings, and all miscellaneous expenses.
Uninsured Motorist	A driver who does not have any liability insurance coverage or a hit-and-run driver who cannot be identified.

Now you are ready to begin the step-into's.

The Step-Into's

By following STEPS ONE through SIX in this chapter you'll be gathering the same information and filing your claim with the insurance company just as a lawyer does. This self-help format gives you the know-how to collect money from the negligent party's insurance company or even your own without using a lawyer. In this way 100 percent of the cash settlement will belong to you. Your recovery will not be reduced because of attorney's fees. Forms and letters follow the step in which they are cited.

- STEP ONE tells how to notify your own insurance company if the accident involves use of your car.

- STEP TWO shows you how to notify the negligent person's liability insurance company (or your own) of an intention to make a claim.

- STEP THREE provides guidelines for gathering all the facts surrounding the accident.

- STEP FOUR gives you the know-how for collecting money damage information.

- STEP FIVE explains how to forward all information to the insurance company.

- STEP SIX gives you the technique for negotiating a cash settlement with the insurance company.

Step One

Notifying Your Own Insurance Company of a Motor Vehicle Accident

When an accidental injury to your property or body happens in connection with use of a motor vehicle such as an automobile, motorcycle, van, truck, or boat, *your own* liability insurer must be notified as soon as possible after the accident.

Whether in a fault or no-fault state, this notification procedure should be carried out. If you don't notify your own carrier, as you are suppposed to under the terms of your insurance policy, not only could your company deny your no-fault, medical payment, collision, or uninsured motorist claim, but it also could deny you coverage for any claim that may be made against you by the other people involved in the accident, leaving you personally responsible.

Use Form 1 to give notice of an accident to your own liability carrier. This should be done immediately.

Form No. 1—Letter to Own Auto Insurance Carrier

DATE:

TO:

     Re: Insured:
           Address:

           Date of Accident:
           Location of Accident:
           Policy Number:

Dear Madam or Sir:

     I am the insured under the above numbered policy of insurance with your company.

     I was involved in an automobile collision on the above date and at the above place and I suffered bodily injury and damages to my motor vehicle.

     I do not know at this time if the other driver has automobile liability coverage.

     This letter will serve as notice under the terms of my policy. If you wish a statement regarding this accident, I can be contacted at the address and telephone number listed below.

Very truly yours,

Address:

Telephone:

Step Two

Notifying the Negligent Party's Insurance Company (or your own) of Intention to Make a Claim

In many cases, you will learn the name of the negligent party's insurance carrier at the time of the accident. However, when this is not possible, a letter must be sent to the negligent party or business requesting this information and/or asking the negligent party to forward your letter to his or her insurance company.

If the negligent person forwards your letter to the insurance carrier, the carrier will, ordinarily, initiate contact with you. Where the other person does not send your letter to the carrier but instead furnishes the carrier's name, it then becomes your responsibility to notify that insurance company of your forthcoming claim.

Where the negligent party is uncooperative and does not furnish the liability carrier's name for you, contact the office of the Secretary of State's insurance division and request this information. If you are still unable to obtain this information, consult with a lawyer.

If your damages have resulted from an auto collision and the other driver, who was the negligent party, has no liability coverage, you must then make a claim under the uninsured motorist provision of your own insurance policy.

Where no-fault liability coverage is in force, and you have been involved in an auto collision, notice of your intention to make a claim must be sent to your own insurance company, as well as to the negligent driver's company if an excess claim against the negligent driver's insurer is a possibility.

Use Form 2 to request the name of the negligent party's liability carrier.

Use Form 3 to notify the negligent party's insurance carrier of your intention to make a claim under the negligent party's policy.

Use Form 4 to notify your own liability insurance carrier of your intention to make a claim under your own policy where the negligent party is an uninsured motorist or a hit-and-run driver.

Use Form 5 to notify your own insurance carrier of your intention to make a claim under your own policy where you have no-fault insurance coverage.

Use Form 6 to request insurance coverage information from your Secretary of State's office.

If you believe that there is more than one person or business responsible for your accident or injury, use the same process and forms for each.

Form No. 2—First Letter to Negligent Party

DATE:

TO:

       Re: Date of Accident:
               Place of Accident:
               Time of Accident:
               Type of Accident:

Dear Madam or Sir:

       Please be advised that I am making a claim against you for my injuries and property damage due to the accident above listed.

       Please notify your insurance company of this matter and send them this letter immediately.

       If you did not have liability insurance on the date of this accident, please contact me either by telephone or by mail at the telephone number and/or address listed below as soon as possible.

       If I do not hear from you or your insurance company within twenty (20) days of the date of this letter, I will be forced to begin legal action against you.

Very truly yours,

Address:

Telephone:

Form No. 3—Letter to Negligent Party's Insurance Company

DATE:

TO:

       Re: Insured Person:
             Address:

             Date of Accident:
             Location of Accident:
             Type of Accident:

Dear Madam or Sir:

Please be advised that your above named insured and I were involved in an incident as above described.

If you have not yet assigned a claim number to this incident, please do so and notify me of same at the address or telephone number listed below.

As soon as I have all items of special damages, I will forward them to you directly.

Very truly yours,

Address:

Telephone:

Form No. 4—Letter to Own Insurance Company Regarding Uninsured Motorist Claim

DATE:

TO:

Re: Insured:
     Policy Number:
     Date of Accident:
     Place of Accident:
     Type of Accident:

Dear Madam or Sir:

Please be advised that regarding the above described accident, I have been informed that the other driver had no liability insurance on the date of this accident.

I am, therefore, making a claim for my injuries under the uninsured motorist provisions of my above numbered policy of insurance.

As soon as I have all items of my special damages, I will forward them directly to you.

Please assign this claim a number and notify me of same at the address or telephone number listed below.

Very truly yours,

Address:

Telephone:

Form No. 5—Letter to Own Liability Carrier for Claim Under No-Fault Policy

DATE:

TO:

Re: Insured:
     Address:

     Policy Number:
     Date of Accident:
     Place of Accident:
     Type of Accident:

Dear Madam or Sir:

    I am the insured under the above numbered policy of insurance with your company.

    I was involved in an automobile collision on the above date and at the above place and I suffered bodily injury and damages to my motor vehicle.

    Please assign this claim a number and notify me at above address.

    As soon as I have all items of special damages, I will forward them you.

Very truly yours,

Address:

Telephone:

Form No. 6—Letter to Secretary of State for Insurance Information Relative to Other Driver

DATE:

TO: Secretary of State
         Financial Responsibility Section

         Re: Date of Accident:
              Location of Accident:

Dear Madam or Sir:

     Please be advised that I was involved in an automobile collision on the above date and at the above location. Please advise me as to whether or not the other driver, as named below, has complied with the financial responsibility laws of your State and if so, how? I have provided the following information to assist you:

Other Driver: _____

Other Driver's Address: _____

Police Department to which
 this accident was
 reported   _____

General Index Number of
 the report   _____

License Number of Other
 Driver
              YEAR   _____

              NUMBER   _____

     Please contact me at the address listed below.

     Thank you for your cooperation and assistance in this matter.

Very truly yours,

Address:

Telephone:

Step Three

Gathering the Facts

A number of sources are available to help you gather an organized record of the accident. You, of course, are the first and foremost source of all the facts surrounding the incident. But you can rely on other, independent sources such as the recollection of any witnesses, the investigative report done by a local police department, photographs taken of the accident scene, physical injuries or damaged property, a diagram of the accident location, and often a weather report furnished by the United States Weather Bureau.

By putting together the information gleaned from the independent sources along with your own personal account of the accident, you are furnishing yourself a full record of an incident whose details will become increasingly vague with the passage of time. You are also providing the insurance adjuster with a thorough version of an unfamiliar event.

Not all sources suggested here will be appropriate or available to you in all cases. Use whatever sources you can and eliminate any sources that don't shed light on your fact situation.

Detailed Account of the Occurrence

As soon as possible after the accident, make a written, voice, or video recording of your version of the incident. If you are physically unable to record these facts yourself, tell them to another person who will record them for you. Include types of facts suggested here, as well as the observations and the sensations you experienced at the time of the accident. This record, if made near to the time of the occurrence, has credibility. The fresher the recollection, the more accurate (and credible) the account is likely to be. This personal factual record will prove useful later on when making a statement to an insurance company or for a court case, if you are unable to negotiate a satisfactory settlement.

The following list offers suggestions only. Feel free to improvise; but include any facts, observations, or sensations that you believe are important. Create as full a picture as possible. If the accidental injury is not connected to an auto or motor vehicle collision, skip over any suggestions here that relate to traffic accident information.

1. Date
2. Location
3. Time
4. Names and addresses of all persons involved
5. Your destination
6. Names and addresses of persons with you
7. Weather conditions
8. Traffic conditions or condition of road, sidewalk, floor, stairs, or other specific accident location
9. Your location immediately before the accident
10. Whether it was a residential or business district
11. Type of roadway, any obstructions, or traffic control signals
12. Lighting conditions
13. Width of street or sidewalk
14. Names and addresses of any witnesses
15. What happened upon impact (or fall)
16. Physical sensations upon impact
17. Conversations immediately after impact
18. Medical treatment initially received, including names and addresses of all persons rendering treatment
19. Name and address of negligent party
20. Description of negligent party's actions or inactions

21. Negligent party's insurance carrier
22. Police report number where applicable and available

Have as much of this information as possible at your fingertips and you'll get off to a good beginning.

A Detailed Account of Bodily Injuries

Where you have been hurt in the accident, a detailed account of your bodily injuries needs to be recorded. This account can be preserved in writing or on audio or video tape. Relate your aches and pains from the time of the accident forward. Use everyday language and stay away from medical or technical terms. Be honest. Don't exaggerate your injury. One of the keys to receiving a reasonable offer from the claims adjuster is your honesty and sincerity.

Keep a diary on a daily basis of all physical or mental pain. When recounting your complaints and injuries, start with a description of your pain, as you remember it, at the scene of the occurrence. Next, move on day by day, describing everything that hurts. Begin with your head and go down through all parts of your body in detail. Explain any problems with each part of your body, such as shooting pain, throbbing pain, or loss of feeling. Include in your record all discomfort since the injury. Medications given at the hospital and afterwards for pain or nervousness should be noted.

Next, relate your injuries, aches, pains, and discomforts to the way you live your life. Take a normal day from the time you rise and shine until the time you go to bed and explain in detail the ways in which the injury has affected or changed your life. For example, describe the changes in the way you put on your clothes, get in and out of bed, take a bath or shower, or move yourself around during the day (or note that you are unable to get around at all).

This personal account of bodily injury will prove a great resource throughout the claim process. Months later, when negotiating your claim settlement with the claims adjuster, a review of this record will bring to mind otherwise forgotten facets of your injury.

A Detailed Account of Property Damage

All personal property items that get damaged or are left unusable need to be listed. Torn clothing, broken eyeglasses, damaged auto, or ruined wristwatch will generate insurance company reimbursement for the cost of the item's repair or its fair market value, whichever is less.

Recent purchase receipts, credit invoices, or cancelled checks should be located and kept with this record.

Where purchase price proof is not available, have independent evaluations made. These can be done by an optometrist for new eyeglasses, a jeweler for a comparable wristwatch, or a clothing store for a similar garment.

If your property can be or is repaired, keep all repair estimates, paid bills, and receipts for loss of use, such as the rental of a substitute automobile.

If your damaged auto can be repaired and the repair costs are less than the car's fair market value, reimbursement will equal your repair costs. But where your repair costs exceed the damaged car's fair market value, reimbursement will be equal only to the fair market value of your automobile. Motor vehicle fair market values are determined by various published guide books in use throughout the insurance industry. They generally are not set by your own independent source.

Your own documentation of all personal property values is important because insurance companies are skeptical of values that are not substantiated.

Photographs

The old saying "a picture is worth a thousand words," is true. Pictures of the accident scene, damaged property, and bodily injuries graphically present your story to the insurance company. Photographs should be saved in case they are necessary years later. Have two sets made — one for you and one for the insurance company's claims adjuster. If you're unable to take pictures, hire a photographer.

When taking pictures of the accident scene, include different views of the location or intersection where the accident occurred, shots of the immediate surrounding area, and skid marks and traffic signals where applicable. If you fell because of a hole in the hall carpeting, a broken hand-railing, or a cracked pavement, record the defect on film.

After the pictures have been developed, write a brief description on the back of each including the date taken and the photographer's name. Mark compass points on all accident scene photos.

All bodily injuries such as bruises, swelling, lacerations, dislocations, breaks, and other obvious injuries need to be photographed in close detail and from different angles. Visible medical treatment to any injuries — casts, slings, or crutches — should also be captured on film. Again, note the date taken on the back of each picture. Your injuries will heal. Pictures don't.

Diagram

Rough out a diagram of the accident location or street intersection so that photographs can be put in perspective. Even if photographs aren't possible, the insurance adjuster can easily determine, from the diagram, the sequence of movement prior to the incident.

Indicate for auto and pedestrian accidents all compass points. Add the location of any traffic control signals, weather conditions, a description of the surrounding area, and visibility conditions. Mark the spot where the accident happened.

If you were involved in a non-auto accident, sketch the staircase, hallway, grocery store aisle, sidewalk, or swimming pool where the accident occurred. Draw the incident's approximate spot, as well as the defect or obstruction causing the accident. Put in all compass points. Where visibility or lighting conditions are important, include these too.

Sometimes a diagram is included in a police report.

Police Report

Often local police are called to the accident scene, whether it is an auto collision, auto-pedestrian knock down, a slip and fall, or even a dog bite incident. The investigating officers question the persons involved, interview any witnesses, and assess all contributing conditions. After the police investigation is completed, a written report is prepared and kept on file with the reporting police department. About one week after the incident, the police department will make this report available.

Order a copy so that you will have access to this information. Certainly the insurance company will have a copy in their file as part of their investigation.

Request a copy of the police report from the city, state, or sheriff's police department that investigated your accident. Form 7 (along with the proper fee) helps you do this. Call beforehand and ask how much the fee is and where to send your request. Allow two weeks for a response. Some local police departments will issue these reports immediately when you request them in person.

Witness Statements

Statements from persons who witnessed the accident, when you are able to get them, offer valuable corroboration of your claim. Witness' names and addresses can be learned at the time of the accident or from the police report and sometimes from the claims adjuster.

Contact each witness, including the negligent party if he or she is agreeable, and take personal statements, if possible. Cover all of the important aspects of the accident. Forms 9, 10, 11, and 12 offer standard questions for witness interviews. Don't be afraid to improvise on these and ask any other questions you believe are significant.

After interviewing the witnesses and writing down their answers, comments, and observations, have them sign the statement including their addresses and telephone numbers for work and home, birth dates, and the interview dates.

If a witness will not consent to an interview in person, carry on the interview over the telephone. Then type up the questions along with the answers and mail it to the witness for signature with a self-addressed, stamped envelope.

Or, if you cannot contact the witness, mail the witness statement form and ask the witness to complete and return it to you. Include a self-addressed, stamped envelope to make it as easy as possible for witnesses to cooperate with you.

Use Form 8 along with the proper witness statement when you can't contact the witness.

Use Form 9 for a witness statement for an automobile collison.

Use Form 10 for a witness statement for a pedestrian accident.

Use Form 11 for a witness statement for a slip and fall accident.

Use Form 12 for a witness statement for a property damage accident.

Uninsured Motorist

When claiming uninsured motorist benefits, your insurance company may request that you prove that the other party did not have insurance on the date of the accident.

This is done by requesting that the uninsured motorist complete a statement indicating that he or she did not have liability coverage on the date of your accident.

Form 13 is used as a cover letter when you're unable to have the uninsured motorist sign this statement in person.

Form 14 is the statement the uninsured motorist must sign.

When this is done by mail, enclose a self-addressed, stamped envelope, making it convenient for the uninsured motorist to help you.

Do not pressure the uninsured motorist. Do not pay for the statement. Your insurance company may independently satisfy itself with respect to this information.

Weather Report

Weather conditions at the time of the accident may reveal or confirm the other person's negligence. Frequently, a driver at fault is going within the speed limit, but going too fast for snowy or rainy conditions. Perhaps a property owner inadequately removed snow or ice accumulations, causing you to fall. Where the weather conditions disclose a fact pointing to the other person's negligence, be sure and get a weather report for the day of the occurrence. The United States Weather Bureau office in your locality will furnish one for a slight charge.

Form No. 7—Accident Report Request

DATE:

To:

Dear Madam or Sir:

Please provide me with a police report for the following described occurrence:

Date: _____

Time: _____

Place: _____

_____

Type of Occurrence: _____

Parties Involved: _____

_____

Enclosed is my check in the sum of $ _____ to cover the cost of this service. Please forward this report to me at the address listed below.

Thank you.

Very truly yours,

ADDRESS:

Form No. 8—Letter to Witness Requesting Statement

Date:

To:

     Re: Date of Accident:
           Place of Accident:

Dear Madam or Sir:

     Your name has been given to me as a witness to the above accident.

     Enclosed please find a Witness Statement, which I would appreciate your completing and returning to me in the enclosed envelope.

     Your statement will help me in my claim for injuries and I would appreciate your assistance.

     Thank you.

Very truly yours,

Form No. 9—Witness Statement for Automobile Collision

S T A T E M E N T

Full Name_____Date of Birth_____

Home Address_____Phone #_____

Work Address_____Phone #_____

Date of Accident:_____Time_____

Place of Accident:_____

Where were you at the time of the accident?_____

Were the street lights lit?_____Were there any traffic lights or signals at

the intersection?_____If so, in whose favor?_____

Describe the vehicles involved (style, color, make license number)_____

_____

In which direction was each vehicle going?_____

What was the speed of each vehicle?_____

Did the vehicles have their headlights on?_____

What was the condition of the streets (dry, wet, icy, snowy)?_____

What was the position of each vehicle after the accident?_____

_____

In your opinion, how did this accident happen?_____

_____

_____

_____

In your opinion, who was at fault and why?_____

_____

Did you hear any comment made by either driver?_____If so, what was

said?_____

Please give the names and addresses of all persons involved._____

_____

Please give the names and addresses of any other witnesses._____

_____

Was a policeofficer present at the time of the accident?_____

Was a policeofficer present after the accident occurred?_____

Signature:_____

Date: _____

Form No. 10—Witness Statement for Pedestrian Accident

S T A T E M E N T

Full Name_____Date of Birth_____

Home Address_____Phone #_____

Work Address_____Phone #_____

Date of Accident:_____Time:_____

Place of Accident:_____

Where were you at the time of the accident?_____

Were the street lights lit?_____Were there any traffic lights or signals at

the intersection?_____If so, in whose favor?_____

Describe the vehicle involved (style, color, make, license number)_____

_____

In which direction was the vehicle going?_____

In which direction was the pedestrian going?_____

What was the speed of the vehicle?_____

Did the vehicle have its headlights on?_____

What was the condition of the streets (dry, wet, icy, snowy)?_____

What part of the vehicle struck the pedestrian?_____

In your opinion, how did this accident happen?_____

_____

_____

_____

In your opinion, who was at fault and why?_____

_____

Did you hear any comment made by either party?_____ If so, what was

said?_____

Please give the names and addresses of all parties involved_____

_____

Please give the names and addresses of any other witnesses_____

_____

Signature;_____

Date:_____

Form No. 11—Witness Statement for Slip & Fall Accident

S T A T E M E N T

Full Name _____ Date of Birth _____

Home Address _____ Phone # _____

Work Address _____ Phone # _____

Date of Accident _____ Time _____

Place of Accident _____

Where were you at the time of the accident? _____

What was the condition of the area at the time of the occurrence? _____

_____

In which direction was the person going at the time of the fall? _____

_____

In your opinion, how did this accident happen? _____

_____

_____

_____

In your opinion, who was to blame and why? _____

_____

Did you hear any comments made as to the cause of the occurrence? _____

If so, what was said? _____

Had you noticed this same condition of the area prior to the accident? ____

If so, for how long? _____

Please give the names and addresses of all persons involved _____

_____

Please give the names and addresses of any other witnesses _____

_____

Signature _____

Date _____

Form No. 12—Witness Statement for Property Damage Accident

<u>S T A T E M E N T</u>

Full Name_____Date of Birth_____

Home Address_____Phone #_____

Work Address_____Phone #_____

Date of Accident_____Time_____

Place of Accident_____

Where were you at the time of this accident?_____

Did you see the condition of the property prior to the damage?_____

If so, what was the condition of the property?_____

In your opinion, describe how the accident happened_____

_____

_____

_____

In your opinion, who or what was to blame?_____

_____

As a result of this accident, what damage was done to the property?_____

_____

Did you see the property owner at the scene of the accident?_____

If so, describe what the owner was doing at the time?_____

_____

Did you hear any comment made by anyone?_____If so, what was said by

whom?_____

Please give the names and addresses of all persons present_____

_____

Please give the names and addresses of any other witnesses_____

_____

Signature _____

Date _____

Form No. 13—Letter to Other Party Requesting Uninsured Motorist Statement

Date:

To:

            Re: Date of Accident:
                  Place of Accident:

Dear Madam or Sir:

     As you have advised me that you did not have insurance on the date of the above accident, I must contact my insurance company for my damage and injury claim.

     Enclosed is a Uninsured Motorist Statement, which I would appreciate your completing, signing and returning to me in the enclosed envelope.

     Your assistance will help me in my claim.

     Thank you.

Very truly yours,

Address:

Telephone:

Form No. 14—Uninsured Motorist Statement

S T A T E M E N T

Full Name_____Date of Birth_____

Home Address_____Phone #_____

Work Address_____Phone #_____

Date of Accident:_____Time_____

Place of Accident:_____

Make of Vehicle:_____Year_____License Plate No._____

Driver's License No._____

    That on the above date and at the above place I was involved in an automobile collision with _____.

    That at the time of this accident I did not have public liability insurance on the vehicle I was driving nor did I have public liability insurance on any other vehicle.

_____
Signature

Date: _____

Step Four

Collecting Information for Money Damages

Now that you've collected the facts, the next step is gathering information that measures your losses. Every sort of economic and non-economic loss suffered because of the accident needs to be authenticated:

- Medical and hospital expenses
- Medical and hospital expenses likely to be incurred in the future
- Value of time, salary, or earnings lost
- Value of time, salary, or earnings likely to be lost in the future
- Cost of repair or value of damaged property
- Pain and suffering
- Disfigurement
- Aggravation of a pre-existing condition
- Miscellaneous expenses

Expenses and loss of earnings must always be reasonable and necessary under the circumstances.

Doctor's Report and Medical Bills

Every doctor or medical professional who has treated your injuries whether in an office, emergency room, or hospital, will furnish a medical report and an itemized medical bill upon request. The medical report will detail the injury diagnosis, treatment given, and prognosis. A fee may be charged for this service.

The doctor's report and itemized treatment bill are necessary when claiming against another's carrier or when claiming under your own policy for uninsured motorist, medical payment, or no-fault payments. Even if your health or hospitalization insurer has paid or reimbursed you for these medical expenses, in many states the negligent party's carrier (and your own, in some instances) is nonetheless responsible. The historic idea being that it is the wrongdoer's obligation to make you whole again in spite of payment from other sources.

For fastest results in getting these items, call the doctor's office and ask if there is a fee for furnishing the report. Then forward a letter and medical report form with the proper fee to each treating doctor or medical professional with a self-addressed, stamped return envelope.

Use form 15 for the cover letter sent to the treating doctors or medical professionals.

Form 16 is the medical report form to be filled out by the treating doctors or medical professionals. Enclose it with Form 15.

Hospital Records and Bills

Where there has been either hospital emergency room treatment or an in-patient stay, the complete hospital record, including x-ray reports, laboratory reports, medical photographs, nurse's notes, doctor's orders, physical therapy records, and the emergency log, must be requested.

These are your records and you are entitled to copies. Before a hospital will release the records, they must have a written request from you with a signed authorization.

Hospital charges are as vital in calculating your economic loss as are medical expenses. Even if hospital costs have been paid for or reimbursed by your health and hospitalization carrier, they are still relevant items of damage when making the claim against the negligent party's carrier or your own for medical payment, uninsured motorist, or no-fault compensation. Request a copy of your hospital bill along with the records.

Photocopy costs or a report fee may be charged.

Use Form 17 to request and authorize a release of your hospital records.

Medical and Hospital Expenses Likely to be Incurred in the Future

An added component to your claim may be the expenses of continuing or additional medical treatment or hospital care. Sometimes these types of expenses can be accurately predicted, such as where a fracture set in a cast has to be checked a certain number of times or plastic surgery needs to be performed on a scar. At other times, these future costs cannot be precisely calculated, such as where ongoing surgeries, nursing care, or physical therapy sessions are required.

Where future medical care costs can be estimated and their necessity verified by your doctor, there is little risk of settling your own claim before these future expenses are incurred.

Make sure your physician, in the medical report, describes any future medical procedures planned, the recuperation period, and any costs. Will there be expenses for a doctor, hospital care, out-patient care, or anesthesia?

On the other hand, if your injury requires a long period of ongoing medical or hospital care, the costs of which are not yet determinable, it would be foolhardy to settle the claim based upon a "guess" of what your future expenses will be. Rather than taking this risk and jeopardizing an otherwise maximum settlement opportunity, consult with an attorney first. You may then wish to retain a lawyer because of these complicating circumstances.

When you hire a lawyer, remember the size of the legal fees may be negotiable given your previous investigative and injury verification work. If a settlement offer has already been made, the lawyer may agree to a contingency fee based on the settlement amount he recovers in excess of the carrier's top written offer to you.

Value of Time, Salary, or Earnings Lost

The accidental injury may keep you from working at your job or in your own business for a period of time. If so, verification of time and earnings lost must be obtained. Salaried employees should have their employers fill out a time lost verification form. Business owners must complete a self-employment affidavit. In both instances, it's necessary to wait until recovery and return to work before having these forms completed.

Lost salaries are recoverable even if sick days or vacation time have been used for the recuperation period.

Self-employed persons claiming finanical losses because of the injury must establish their credibility. Along with the self-employment affidavit, the business owner should attach a copy of the prior year's federal income tax return indicating net business income.

Use Form 18 for the cover letter that is sent with the Time Lost Verification Form.

Use Form 19 for the Time Lost Verification.

Use Form 20 for the Self-Employment Loss of Earnings Affidavit or statement.

Value of Time, Salaries, or Earnings Likely to be Lost in the Future

Injuries that keep you from working for a long time period increase your economic loss and therefore the size of your claim. Where proof of wages or income likely to be lost in the future can be calculated with certainty, this aspect of your claim can confidently be given to the insurance carrier for settlement consideration.

This may happen when additional one-time surgeries or periodic check-ups of healing fractures can be predicted. The time you will lose from work in these types of instances can readily be figured into the damage claim.

Where you are self-employed, add to the value of time lost, the cost, if any, of additional help that must be hired while you are undergoing the medical procedure and recuperation.

Where proof of future lost time values require sophisticated mathematical projections or cannot be calculated due to the ongoing nature of the disability, an informed settlement demand can't be made. Because of the risk of settling the claim too low and the chance of insurance company rejection if your demand is too high, it's best in this instance to consult a lawyer.

Earnings likely to be lost in the future, whether they are predictable with certainty or not, must always be confirmed in writing by your treating doctor. Ask your doctor to describe, in writing, the future medical procedures or care required and the estimated amount of time needed for the procedure and recovery.

Cost of Repair or Value of Damaged Property

Dollar for dollar insurance company reimbursement in the damaged or destroyed property area is the cost of repair or the value of damaged property, whichever is less.

When making a motor vehicle collision claim with your own insurance carrier, expect payment to follow this general rule – fair market value or cost of repairs, whichever is less. From this figure the company will subtract your policy deductible.

Property damage costs, when they are paid by another's carrier, can include not only the repair or replacement value of your auto, but also the repair or replacement costs of any personal property damaged in the accident. Reasonable and necessary expenses for loss of the property's use, such as for an auto rental while your car is being fixed, may be recovered from another's insurer. Generally these are not recoverable under your own policy unless you have purchased this specific kind of insurance.

With respect to property values, it is always up to you, except in the automobile category, to establish and authenticate the value of destroyed property. In order to determine the value of destroyed, or personal property, find all purchase receipts, cancelled checks, or charge account invoices to substantiate purchase prices for any sporting goods, lost contact lenses, jewelry, or other property destroyed in the accident. Where you have no access to this type of proof, obtain independent evaluations from the sports store, optometrist, jeweler, or other purveyor of the type of property destroyed. Evaluations should be in writing. This way you establish the property's retail or replacement value in support of your claim.

You probably will find wide discrepancies between estimates for property repairs. Take the time to get two estimates of repair for all items that can be fixed, including your auto. Make sure the estimates include all work that needs to be done because of the accident. Estimates should include the cost of top quality and not second hand parts, as well as labor done by professionally trained persons who will do a first rate repair job.

When it comes to an automobile, the insurance company always sets the value based upon published tables in use throughout the insurance industry. Again, where the cost of repair exceeds the car's value, the company will pay you this book value. In contrast, where the cost of repair is less than the car's value, you'll receive the cost of the repair.

Pain and Suffering

When you have suffered bodily injury, you are entitled to receive additional compensation for the pain and suffering you've experienced.

Although no exact formula can be used for calculating pain and suffering compensation, serious injuries such as fractures, justify a higher settlement than pulled muscle injuries. Permanent injuries too, like facial scarring and the loss of the use of an arm or hand, presume more pain and suffering than quick healing injuries like cuts, bruises, and sprains.

Because pain and suffering is difficult to measure and hard to accurately describe to another, the personal bodily injury record compiled in STEP THREE will crystalize the pain and suffering factor for both you and the insurance adjuster. These recorded experiences and observations along with a compatible medical report, will give added credibility to a settlement demand that may substantially exceed your actual money damages.

Be fair and honest with the adjuster when advancing your claim for pain and suffering. If you are alleging severe pain from low back pains over an eight month period and sought medical attention only twice, your agony will be hard to believe.

On the other hand, if the pain lingers for a long time, seek medical attention. Not only will this physically help you, but will substantiate the pain and suffering claimed.

The doctor may tell you that your low back condition will be permanent and recurring resulting in surgery and more time away from work. If so, have the doctor include this prognosis in the written report. In that way, the pain and suffering you've experienced will be believeable to the insurance adjuster.

Disfigurement

You are entitled to reasonable compensation for any disfigurement to your body caused by the accidental injury. Disfigurements can include a fractured finger that heals in a crooked way, a scar from the accident itself or from resulting surgery, or skin discolored from a burn.

As with pain and suffering, the money value of a disfigurement is difficult to measure, there being no readily available formula. A one inch scar on the top of your foot does not call for the same compensation were the scar on your face. Conversely, the same one inch scar on your foot is worth substantially more compensation if you modeled shoes or hosiery for your livelihood.

Where there is a scar or any kind of disfigurement, your doctor must include mention of this in his report. He should also describe the disfigurement in detail. Is the scar raised or flat? Can it be revised? Is it discolored? Is it permanent? If any future medical treatment is planned, such as plastic surgery, the doctor should note the estimated medical, hospital, and anesthesia costs, as well as the length of time you'll have to be away from your job.

Disability

If you are left with a disability caused by the accident, whether temporary or permanent, this too, is an element of your damage compensation claim. As with pain and suffering or disfigurement, there is no ready measure upon which to base a value.

A housewife who takes care of a family and fractures bones in the hand, forcing her to be in a cast for a month, has a greater disability than a fifth grade student suffering the same injury. Yet more compensation would be due the professional piano player who is prevented from earning a living because of a similar disability.

Where the disability is of a more permanent nature and interferes with the way you earn your living, the compensation will be even greater. A surgical nurse left with permanent numbness in her hand after an auto accident can no longer perform the ordinary functions of her job. This type of permanent disability keeps her from ever again performing her professional duties and therefore justifies substantial disability compensation.

Your doctor's report must confirm the nature of the disability and describe how it interferes with your employment tasks, either for a limited or permanent time.

Aggravation of a Pre-existing Condition

Many people believe that they cannot receive compensation for accidental injuries caused by another's negligence where the recent injury merely complicates or aggravates a present condition or ailment. Not so. The right to compensation where further injury is caused by another's negligence is well recognized by insurance companies.

An example of a damage claim for aggravation of a pre-existing condition is the man, who over a four year period, has injured his back several times at work while lifting heavy bundles. Because of these repeated injuries, his back is left in a weakened condition. When leaving a friend's apartment, he slips and falls on a loose stair, reinjuring his back. He can recover for all losses and expenses caused by the fall including compensation for aggravation of his pre-existing back injury.

This same idea holds true for the woman whose arthritic hip is broken after being struck by a car. Her recovery will be occasioned by significantly more pain and suffering and will take longer to heal because her hip had already been arthritic. Consequently, her pain and suffering claim will exceed that which is ordinarily occasioned by this sort of injury.

Your doctor's report along with prior medical or hospital records verifying aggravation of the pre-existing condition or ailment must accompany your claim. Prior records can be obtained in the same way and at the same time current ones are requested.

Miscellaneous Expenses

Other items of special damage normally included in the settlement demand are listed here. In order for your miscellaneous expenses to have authenticity, keep all receipts, paid bills, repair estimates, property replacement valuation, and insurance confirmations for forwarding to the insurance company. Some of these include:

1. Emergency room charges
2. Ambulance service
3. Medicar service
4. X-rays
5. Prescriptions
6. Car rentals
7. Physical therapy bills
8. Cost of trips for doctor, hospital, or physical therapist visits
9. Nursing expenses
10. Housekeeping expenses
11. Brace, collar, wheelchair, or crutches expenses
12. Clothing loss, repair, or cleaning
13. Eyeglasses replacement
14. Help needed in your business where you are self-employed and can't work.

This is by no means an exhaustive list, but it can help you recognize that each and every expense reasonably related to property damage, bodily injury, or loss of earnings can be recovered.

Form No. 15—Letter to Treating Doctor Requesting Report

DATE:

TO:

      Re: Patient:
             Address:
             Date of Birth:
             Date of Accident:

Dear Dr.

      Please furnish to me at your earliest possible convenience a complete medical report indicating your diagnosis and prognosis of the injuries for which you have recently treated me.

      Enclosed is a Medical Report Form for your convenience, along with your fee for this report and a self-addressed, stamped envelope.

      Please also include a copy of your itemized billing for your treatment to me up to this date.

      Your cooperation will be appreciated.

Very truly yours,

PHONE:

Form No. 16—Medical Report Form

<u>MEDICAL REPORT</u>

Patient Name: _____ Address: _____

Date of Accident: _____

History:

Subjective Symptoms:

Objective Findings:

X-Ray or Test Results:

Diagnosis:

Treatment:

Prognosis:

Dates of Treatment:

Amount of Bill for Services Rendered:

_____
Signature of Physician

_____
Address

Date of Report:

Form No. 17—Letter Requesting Hospital Records

Date:

To:

        Re: Patient:
             Address:
             Date of Birth:
             Date of Treatment:
             Date of Accident:
             Social Security No.

Dear Madam or Sir:

      I hereby request that you forward to me complete copies of all of the hospital records, including x-ray reports, itemized billing, surgery reports, emergency room reports, physical therapy records and any other documents relative to your hospital's treatment of me on the above stated date.

      Enclosed please find my check in the sum of $_____ to cover the cost of this service.

      Kindly forward these documents to me at the address listed below.

      Your cooperation and prompt attention to this request will be appreciated.

Very truly yours,

Address:

Telephone:

Form No. 18—Letter to Employer Requesting Time Lost from Work

Date:

To:

Re: Employee:
      Address:
      Social Security Number:

Dear Madam or Sir:

Would you be kind enough to complete the enclosed Lost Time Verification form pertaining to my recent accident and my absence from work.

I am enclosing a self-addressed, stamped envelope for your convenience.

Your cooperation and prompt attention to this request will be greatly appreciated.

Very truly yours,

Form No. 19—Time Lost Form to be Sent to Employer

TIME LOST VERIFICATION

Name of Employer _____

Address _____Phone # _____

Name of Employee _____

Address _____Phone # _____

Date Employed: _____

Time Lost From work
(regardless whether or not
  employee was paid)   FROM_____TO_____Inclusive
                                       Date   Date

Average Salary $_____Per_____

Bonus, Commissions or overtime
  lost, if any $_____

Employee's Regular Duties   _____

_____

Comments: _____

_____

_____

Signed_____

Title _____

Date _____

Form No. 20—Lost Time Affidavit for Self-Employed

STATE OF ILLINOIS   )
) SS
COUNTY OF COOK   )

<u>A F F I D A V I T</u>

_____, being first duly sworn on oath deposes and states as follows:

    I.   That I reside at: _____

_____;

    2.   That on _____ I was involved in an accident which occurred at or near _____

_____;

    3.   That as a result of said accident I was unable to work from _____ to _____;

    4.   That at the time of the accident I was self-employed under the business name of _____

located at _____

and my weekly earnings were $ _____;

    5.   That because I was unable to work I lost income in the amount of $ _____.

Signature _____

DATE:_____

Subscribed and sworn to
before me this _____ day
of _____,19__.

_____
Notary Public

Step Five

Sending Information to the Insurance Company

Now that you've collected all the facts suggested in STEP THREE and all the special damage information called for in STEP FOUR, you are ready to organize the materials and send them off with a detailed cover letter to the insurance carrier.

An organized presentation is important to insurance adjusters. You can't blame them. The adjuster can only learn about your accident and injuries from the information you submit. Therefore, materials put together in a slipshod manner will be difficult to understand and create obstacles for the adjuster and for you ultimately. Make the claim adjuster's job easy. Give a good first impression. This approach will help your claim.

Use Form 21 to send photocopies of your accident diagram, photographs, police reports, medical reports, hospital records, or weather reports that support your claim. Attach them to Form 21 in the same order listed.

If you are making a claim under the uninsured motorist provision of your own policy, list the uninsured motorist statement (Form 14) as one of your supporting materials in Form 21.

Next, use Forms 22, 23, 24, or 25 to itemize all personal injury and lost income damages. Total these up. Then itemize all your property damages and total these up. These are your dollar for dollar damage amounts.

Attach all documents in support of your damage claim, such as paid bills, repair estimates, hospital bills, self-employment affidavit or employer's lost time verification, medical bills, and miscellaneous expenses in the same order listed in your cover letter.

The adjuster would be truly impressed if all of your information was enclosed in a plastic cover with a removable binder.

Do not send your personal accounts of bodily injury or property damage. Keep these handy though. They will be useful when negotiating the claim settlement amount with the adjuster.

Use Form 22 when sending this information to the negligent party's insurance company.

Use Form 23 when sending the information to your own carrier to support an uninsured motorist claim.

Use Form 24 only when medical payment expenses are sought from your own insurance carrier.

Use Form 25 when making a no-fault claim with your own insurance carrier.

You may be submitting Form 24 for medical pay to your own insurance company at the same time as you are submitting Form 22 to the negligent party's carrier.

In addition, you may be submitting Form 22 to more than one insurance company at the same time. This is where you are injured or your property is damaged by more than one negligent person. Your damage claim must then be sent to all negligent parties' insurance companies. This can happen when two cars collide at an intersection and one of them strikes your car. Both drivers and, consequently, both their insurance companies are responsible. Although you cannot collect the full value of your loss from each company, you must make a claim against all possibly negligent parties so that you will not end up with a lower total settlement.

Form No. 21—Letter to Insurance Carrier with Investigation Documents

DATE:

TO:

      Re: Insured:
            Claimant:
            Date of Accident:
            Claim Number:

Dear Madam or Sir:

      I am enclosing the following investigation documents to support my claim for the above accident:

1. _____ ;
2. _____ ;
3. _____ ;
4. _____ ;
5. _____ ;
6. _____ ;
7. _____ .

      Also, enclosed are all of my items of special damages as of the date of this letter.

Very truly yours,

Address:

Telephone:

Form No. 22—Letter to Negligent Party's Insurance Company with Items of Special Damages

DATE:

TO:

        Re: Insured:
              Claimant:
              Date of Accident:
              Claim Number:

Dear Madam or Sir:

Enclosed please find the following items of special damages regarding the above accident:

        _____ $_____

        _____   _____

        _____   _____

        _____   _____

        _____   _____

        _____   _____

        _____   _____

        _____

Total Medical and Lost Time $_____

        _____   _____

        _____   _____

        _____   _____

Total Property Damage $_____

Please review these items and I will contact you if I do not hear from you within two weeks from the date of this letter.

I hope we can resolve this matter amicably. Thank you.

Very truly yours,

Address:

Telephone:

Form No. 23—Letter to Own Insurance Carrier for Uninsured Motorist Claim with Items of Special Damages

DATE:

TO:

        Re: Insured:
              Date of Accident:
              Policy Number:

Dear Madam or Sir:

In accordance with the uninsured motorist provisions of my above numbered policy, enclosed please find the following items of special damages relative to my injuries:

_____ $_____

_____   _____

_____   _____

_____   _____

_____   _____

_____   _____

_____   _____

Total Medical and Lost Time $_____

_____   _____

_____   _____

_____   _____

Total Property Damage $_____

Please review these items and I will contact you if I do not hear from you within two weeks from the date of this letter.

I hope we can resolve this matter amicably. Thank you.

Very truly yours,

Address:

Telephone:

Form No. 24—Letter to Own Insurance Carrier for Medical Expense Reimbursement with Items of Medical Damages

Date:

To:

      Re: Insured:
            Date of Accident:
            Medical Payment Claim No.
            Policy Number:

Dear Madam or Sir:

      In accordance with the Medical Payment Provisions of my above numbered policy of insurance, enclosed please find the following items of medical special damages:

_____	$ _____
_____	_____
_____	_____
_____	_____
_____	_____
Total	$ _____

      After you have reviewed my claim, kindly forward your draft for reimbursement of these items to me at the address listed below.

Very truly yours,

Address:

Telephone:

Form No. 25—Letter to Own Insurance Carrier Under No-Fault with Items of Special Damages

DATE:

TO:

Re: Insured:
    Date of Accident:
    Claim Number:
    Policy Number:

Dear Madam or Sir:

Please be advised that I am making a claim for damages under the no fault provisions of my above captioned policy. Notice of the occurrence was sent to you on _____.

Enclosed please find the following items of special damages:

_____	$_____
_____	_____
_____	_____
_____	_____
_____	_____
_____	_____
Total Medical and Lost Time	$_____
_____	_____
_____	_____
_____	_____
_____	_____
Total Property Damage	$_____

Please review these items and I will contact you if I do not hear from you within two weeks from the date of this letter.

I hope we can resolve this matter amicably. Thank you.

Very truly yours,

Address:

Telephone:

Step Six

Settling the Claim with the Insurance Company

You have reached the important finale – negotiating a fair cash settlement with the insurance company. But before you plunge in, here are a few suggestions to help you succeed.

You've already been cautioned that insurance company adjusters do not respond well to a sloppy or disorganized claim presentation. Experience has also shown that adjusters are equally unresponsive to hostility and belligerence. Your approach with the claims adjuster ought to be that of a salesperson – familiar with your product, aware of what it's worth and able to communicate this information to the adjuster in a friendly, but businesslike way. Bring the adjuster over to your side.

Remember too, that not all insurance claim amounts are negotiable. Only where there is bodily injury will you be given the benefit of compensation for intangible injuries, in addition to reimbursement of your out-of-pocket expenses.

The negotiable opportunity arises most frequently when the injury claim is made against the negligent person's liability carrier. It may also present itself when you are claiming under the uninsured motorist provisions of your own auto policy.

In all other situations, such as for medical payment, property damage, and no-fault claims without excess damages, your settlement amount is generally not negotiable. You are entitled to reimbursement only – that is, a fixed amount based upon your actual expenses or losses incurred within the limits of the insurance policy under which the claim is being made.

Where there are negotiation possibilities, the settlement amount can range anywhere between two and one-half to four times or more of the total amount of your actual injury expenses, plus property damage reimbursement. The multiplier is used to compensate you for the intangible or general damages you may have suffered, such as pain and suffering, disfigurement, disability, or permanency of the injury.

Compensation or reimbursement for personal injury and property damage does not, under Internal Revenue provisions, have to be included in your gross income. The reason behind this is that any money received whether by lawsuit or settlement for personal injuries or property damage is not considered enrichment. It's only to make you whole again.

Before taking a closer look at the guidelines for making a settlement demand, a last bit of preliminary advice is offered. Prior to attempting the settlement, be familiar with your facts and figures. It may have been many months since the accident or any medical treatment. Review your materials. Make sure your arithmetic is correct. Reread your personal bodily injury and property damage accounts. Have all information at your fingertips when you make the telephone call to the adjuster. Decide on an opening demand figure and the lowest one acceptable to you, before you begin negotiating.

Now, let's take a closer look at the guidelines for negotiating a settlement.

Guidelines for Negotiating a Settlement Claim

Settlement amounts are open to negotiation in these situations:

1.   For all personal injuries resulting from an auto accident in fault states.

2.   For all personal injuries resulting from a non-auto related accident in all states.

3.   For all personal injuries resulting from an auto accident caused by an uninsured motorist in fault states and for some personal injuries resulting from an auto accident caused by an uninsured motorist in no-fault states.

4.   For all personal injuries resulting from an auto accident and not compensated for under your own no-fault auto policy when this is allowed under your state's no-fault law.

In all these instances, compensation is generally based upon a combination of your special and general damages (including the value of your lost time). Then, a multiplier is applied in lieu of any exact measure for intangible injuries such as pain and suffering, disability, disfigurement, or permanency. Next, after multiplied, all property damage costs or values are added to the total, giving you a gross figure.

The multiplier number used depends on the custom in your state and the degree of intangible damages. For example, in some states, the customary rule for settlement is three times your special damages plus all property damages. In other states, the customary multiplier may be as low as two and one-half or as high as four times your special damages. And too, a higher multiplier is used where the intangible injuries are significant. The multiplier can go up as high as four or five or even ten when extreme pain and suffering, disfigurement, disability, or permanency are involved.

Although this same multiplier technique is used in states where comparative fault is used to determine fair compensation in accident cases, the entire claim demand, including your property damage amounts, will be reduced by a percentage equal to the amount of negligence that was attributable to you. Where comparative fault is used, you have an opportunity to negotiate the percentage of your negligence. Therefore, if the negligent party's carrier believes, from their investigation, and you agree,that you were 25 percent responsible for the accident, your claimed amount of all damages, including property reimbursement costs, will be reduced by 25 percent.

Property damage claims, except for the one instance just described, are generally reimbursed on a dollar for dollar basis. No multiplier is used. The negligent party's carrier, as well as your own, pays only the fair market value of the property or the cost of repairs, whichever is less. Therefore, if the fair market value of your 1975 Ford is $800, according to the insurance company's value tables, and the costs of repairs is $4,000, it is the lesser amount or fair market value of $800 that you will receive.

Property damages can be claimed under the uninsured motorist provisions of your own policy if this kind of coverage has been purchased. Before adding any personal property to your uninsured motorist claim, check your policy.

Guidelines When Claim is Made under No-Fault Policies

Settling a claim with your own auto liability carrier under a no-fault policy is not a negotiable opportunity. No multipliers are used to measure compensation for intangible injuries and no negligence percentage reducers are used to diminish the reimbursement allowed under the policy.

Each state that has a no-fault system of auto liability reimbursement has it's own unique payment rules. It is your individual no-fault insurance policy that informs you of your compensation limits in each category of damage. For example, your policy may limit the total reimbursement for medical and hospital costs and loss of earnings to $25,000. Further limitations may apply in each payment category. There may be a reimbursement restriction on lost earnings, for example, of $1,000 per month with payment extending no longer than three years. It is also possible that loss of earnings reimbursement may be limited to $125 per week or not reimbursed at all until you've been off work for longer than one week. Medical expenses too, may have differing dollar limits and time period prohibitions.

Some no-fault plans further restrict benefits by paying economic losses or injury damages only in excess of money you receive from outside sources such as salary continuation plans, pension plans, health insurance or unemployment benefits.

Notwithstanding a no-fault auto insurance compensation plan, you can still, in most no-fault states, and in many circumstances, make a claim against the negligent driver's liability carrier for compensation of general damages. Here are some representative examples taken from several different state's no-fault laws of when an excess claim can be made. You must check with your own insurance agent to know which of these open up an excess claim opportunity for you.

- For excess medical, dental or hospital expenses not covered in your no-fault policy.
- For excess lost earnings not covered in your no fault policy.
- When bodily injuries include a fractured bone or a fractured weight bearing bone.
- When you sustain a permanent intangible injury, such as loss of a body function, permanent disability, disfigurement, or significant scarring.
- If there is death of a family member.
- Where you suffer loss of a body part.
- When you have lost wages or income for a specific number of days.
- Where your medical expenses arc more than a threshold amount set out in your policy.

Where an excess claim is possible under your state's no-fault laws, you will be able to negotiate a settlement when multipliers and sometimes negligence percentage reducers are used.

Guidelines for Medical Payment or Property Damage Claims

Medical payment expenses, whether made against another's homeowner policy or under your own auto liability policy, are always reimbursed on a dollar for dollar basis. Generally, there's a maximum per person per incident dollar amount limit. There also may be a deductible amount subtracted from the medical payment reimbursement.

Property damage reimbursement is also fairly cut and dry. The same set of rules apply whether seeking reimbursement from your own or another person's carrier. You can only receive the fair market value or the repair costs, whichever is less. This amount may be reduced by a deductible when claiming against your own carrier. It is not subject to a deductible when made against another's insurer.

An auto damage claim is an example of when a deductible is used. If the fair market value of your auto is $5,500, repairs total $6,500 and your deductible is $500.00, you receive $5,000 from your own carrier. The same claim made against another's carrier will net you the auto's full fair market value of $5,500.

Additionally, you may receive, either under your own policy, if this coverage has been purchased, or against the negligent party's insurance company, other reasonable and necessary expenses related to the loss of use of your auto, such as travel expenses, car rental costs (subject to a maximum dollar amount), and emergency towing service.

Besides auto damage and its loss of use, claims made against another's company can also include personal property items like a torn suit or raincoat, damaged luggage, or even dentures.

You cannot, however, collect property damage twice—once from the other person's carrier and again from your own.

Negotiating A Claim with the Adjuster

Settlement negotiations may be handled by telephone, letter, or a face-to-face meeting. Usually, the insurance adjuster's case load requires that these negotiations be done by telephone.

If after mailing your claim letter and information to the carrier you have not heard from an adjuster in 20 days or so, contact him by phone. If you don't know the adjuster assigned to your case, give the switchboard operator the claim number, insured person's name and date of the accident. The operator will connect you.

First, with all your information before you, including your detailed accounts of the accident, bodily injuries, and property damage, check with the adjuster to make sure your package of information arrived. If so, start out by discussing the facts surrounding the accident. The other party may have given a somewhat different version of the accident. Find out where you agree and where you disagree. Learn what the differences are. It's alright if the other person's version differs from yours in small ways. Minor differences will not affect the claim. In contrast, if the witness statements or police reports don't support your story and you have no other independent support, your compensation will be reduced because of these significant discrepancies.

Once it is clear under which facts the adjuster is operating, you can move on to the next order of business—going over with the adjuster each item of damage and expense in each category, such as doctor bills, dental bills, future medical bills, hospital costs, lost earnings, property damage, property replacement, and miscellaneous expenses. Make sure you agree on the nature of all damages sustained and the expenses incurred for each item.

Next, tell the adjuster that based upon all the facts and based upon the kinds of injuries and damages you've suffered, you are willing to settle the claim for whatever amount you believe the claim to be fairly worth. Using your detailed accounts of the accident, bodily injuries, and property damage, bring to the adjuster's attention all the facts that lend strength to your evaluation. Give an opening settlement demand at the high range of your multiplied calculations.

The example that follows shows all items of damage, all expenses and a demand range of $5,200 to $7,500 based upon multipliers of approximately two and one-half and four times the special damage amount including property damage.

EXAMPLE

SPECIAL DAMAGES

Doctor bills	$ 495.00	
Physical therapy	165.00	
Emergency room	85.00	
X-rays	120.00	
Lost earnings	700.00	

TOTAL SPECIAL DAMAGES	$1,565.00	$1,565.00
Multiple for pain and suffering, disfigurement, disability and/or permanency	X 2.5	X 4
Total special damages multiplied by intangible injuries	$3,912.50	$6,260.00

PROPERTY DAMAGE

Auto repair	$1,200.00	$1,200.00
Broken eyeglasses	85.00	85.00
Total all Property Damages	$1,285.00	$1,285.00

Approximate Settlement Range (total of special, intangible and property damage)	$5,197.20	to	$7,545.00
Opening Settlement Demand			$7,500.00

Open with a settlement demand of $7,500, a rounded figure based on a multiple at the high end of the settlement range. At this point the adjuster may say your demand is too high based upon certain weaknesses in your case. A counteroffer may be made discounting your demand because the adjuster believes, from investigation, that your actions or inactions contributed to cause the accident. Or, maybe the adjuster will accept your settlement demand. Whatever transpires, listen carefully to the reasons should an adjuster want to reduce your opening settlement demand. Know beforehand the rock bottom figure you'll accept. If the adjuster's reasons for the counteroffer or reduced settlement amount make sense to you *and* this amount is within your approximate settlement range, then accept it, settling your case. Keep in mind that by accepting a settlement at this stage, you are not only avoiding legal fees of one third or more on the compensation amount, but are also eliminating what may be a several year wait for trial, as well as the extra costs of going to trial. That too is worth dollars.

On occasions, negotiations with the adjuster may continue through several more phone conversations or face-to-face meetings. Eventually, you'll receive a final or best offer. If this offer is not acceptable to you because you believe it does not reasonably compensate you for your damages, ask the adjuster to put the final offer in writing. Then consult a lawyer specializing in personal injury work for an opinion. Bring all your information, including the insurance company's top offer. Ask the lawyer for an opinion on the value of your claim. You need not, at this point, mention any offers you've received. Also, ask the lawyer how long it will be before your case goes to trial, what the trial preparation costs will be, and what the legal fees will be. If the lawyer wants to study your papers before giving you an opinion, make copies. Don't leave your originals. It's advisable to go through this process with two different lawyers who specialize in this area of the law. Give each the same information and ask each the same questions.

If, after thinking it over or consulting with a lawyer, you decide to accept the offer, contact the adjuster. Releases will be sent to you. Once the signed releases are received by the insurance company, a settlement check for the agreed amount will be sent to you.

On the other hand, if you decide to hire a lawyer to represent you, inform the adjuster of your decision. Contact a lawyer and negotiate a contingent fee. The lawyer may agree to charge a fee only on the amount recovered over the insurance company's top offer.

This same negotiation process should be used in all instances with an insurance adjuster when multipliers are applied to personal injury expenses for intangible injury compensation. This also holds true when you are negotiating a claim in a no-fault state for an excess amount against the negligent driver's carrier. The settlement process as illustrated before is again appropriate.

The kinds and amounts of injury items claimed against the negligent driver's liability carrier or even your own when making an uninsured motorist claim in a no-fault state, depend on state law and the provisions of your insurance policy.

The following example, based on hypothetical no-fault state laws, illustrates when dollar for dollar reimbursement is available in an excess claim and when an excess claim demand can include the use of a multiplier.

No-fault state laws allow an excess reimbursement claim when your medical bills are over $500 and the value of your lost time exceeds $1,200. However, if you have suffered a broken bone in the accident, a claim can be made not only for your excess financial losses, but also for any intangible injuries, such as pain and suffering.

Therefore, if your medical bills are $650, your lost time is valued at $1,500, and you have sustained only bumps and bruises and no broken bones in the accident, your excess claim against the negligent driver's carrier is only for $450. No multipliers are used and $450 is the full amount of your settlement demand and reimbursement. ($150 excess medical and $300 excess for loss of earnings.)

If, however, you have broken a bone and have incurred the exact same financial losses of $650 for medical and $1,500 for lost time, your demand against the negligent driver's carrier is no longer limited to reimbursement of the $450. To this figure, a multiplier representing the intangible injury of pain and suffering will be applied. Your settlement demand will then be subject to negotiation.

In order to know when the excess claim can be made only for reimbursement and when it can include compensation that takes into account any intangible injuries, you must read your state's no-fault law and your insurance policy. All the answers will be there.

Settling a Claim for Property Damage, No-Fault Policy Benefits, and Medical Payments

Since payment for property damage, medical expenses, and no-fault benefits represents dollar for dollar reimbursement of actual expenses only, the process of settling in these instances is generally uneventful. Unless there's some problem, chances are you won't even converse with an adjuster once your claim letter and bills have been sent to the insurance company. After your information is processed by the insurance company, a release or proof of loss form and a check for the claimed amount will be routinely sent.

With respect to your no-fault claim, if there is some difficulty with it, the claims adjuster will contact you. Further loss documentation may be necessary. If so, the insurance company representative will specify the additional verification needed. Once you've furnished the additional materials, a settlement based upon actual damages within your policy limits will be complete. Releases will then be sent to you. When the signed releases are received by the company, a settlement check will be sent for the settled amount.

Medical payment claims are also reimbursed on a dollar for dollar basis subject to your policy limit. Unless the insurance company has a question regarding some aspect of the claim, a release or proof of loss and reimbursement check by the insurer will be forwarded to you. However, a deductible amount may be subtracted from the medical payment reimbursement.

Property damage claims are similarly handled by the insurance company in a routine way. These, generally, are not negotiable events.

When claiming under your own auto collision provisions, reimbursement represents the fair market value of the damaged auto or its repair costs, whichever is less. From this amount, a deductible is subtracted before reimbursement is given. A deductible is not subtracted when a property damage claim is made against the negligent person's insurance company. Reimbursement for property damage, however, may be reduced where applicable by the percentage of negligence attributable to you.

After the property damage claim is received, the insurance company will forward releases to you and thereafter a settlement check. Again, if there are any obstacles to your settlement demand, an insurance adjuster or your agent will contact you.

Obstacles can arise where the repair bills submitted exceed the property's value as seen through the insurance company's eyes. Or the company may ask you to get a second repair estimate, if yours seems too high. Furnish any additional information requested so that the claim can be paid.

If, on the other hand, you have not heard or received anything in response to your claim letter after three weeks, telephone the adjuster or your agent.

In most cases, property damages claims, if properly documented, are paid by insurance companies without delay.

Giving a Statement to the Insurance Company

Sometime after the accident, but before settlement, the insurance adjuster you are dealing with may ask you to make a statement. Occasionally this is done in person, but usually it's taken over the telephone and taped by the insurance company.

The statement usually consists of your responses to questions asked by the adjuster regarding the accident and your injuries and damages.

This is standard procedure. Straightforward responses are all that is needed. It's to your benefit to cooperate. Many insurers won't pay a claim unless a statement is made to them.

Now is the time to refer to the detailed accounts of the occurrence, bodily injuries, and property damage. Read each of these over before giving your statement. Use them freely during the statement taking process. It's alright to let the adjuster know you have these accounts and are using them to refresh your recollection of events.

Answer truthfully. Don't exaggerate your injuries. Stick to the facts. Chances are the insurance company has already made an independent investigation of the accident and your injuries. One small exaggeration or hedge on the truth will affect your credibility and jeopardize the whole negotiation process. Use this opportunity to put your best foot forward.

Releases

Before your claim settlement check will be issued, the insurance company will ask you to sign a release or "proof of loss form." Occasionally, the release is supplied on the back of the settlement check. This way, your endorsement also serves as a release.

By signing the release, you are letting the negligent party and his insurance company "off the hook" in exchange for the settlement amount you've accepted. The release acts to protect the wrongdoer and the insurance company from any future claims for the same injury or damage. The same kinds of releases, for the same kinds of reasons, are also necessary when a claim is settled with your own insurance carrier.

Most state laws regarding releases are very strict. Ordinarily, a case cannot be reopened once the release is signed. Be sure you are satisfied with the settlement before you sign it. Read it through a couple of times. Understand who is being released and what kind of claim you are releasing. Is it medical pay? Is it property damage? Is it for personal injuries?

If you are receiving compensation for either property damage or personal injury only, make certain the release clearly reflects this. It would be incorrect under these circumstances for the release to say, "all claims."

If you are releasing a medical payment claim, the release must say that payment is for *"medical payment"* only, and not "all claims".

Where two or more persons or businesses caused your injury or damage at the same time, do not release both unless that is your intention. For instance, if while leaving a shopping center, you slipped and fell on a mound of snow in the parking lot that had been negligently plowed by a snow removal company, both the shopping center and snow removal company are responsible for your injuries. Each is responsible to the extent of its fault. If the settlement is only from the shopping center and the claim is still pending with the snow removal company, sign a release naming only the shopping center (and its insurance carrier). Do not sign a release naming "all parties" or one also naming the snow removal company.

The same kind of situation can come about if you are a passenger in a car that's involved in an intersection collision with another car. Both drivers may be at fault. Both may be responsible for your damages depending upon their relative degrees of fault. If you've settled your claim against one driver, don't sign a release in favor of both drivers or "all parties".

In some states, a release as to one person will automatically release all persons responsible for the damage or injury. Consult an attorney to find out if such laws exist in your state. Where multiple parties contributed to your injuries or damages, the insurance adjuster can supply the appropriate document releasing one person without releasing everyone else responsible.

Where a settlement has been made under a no-fault auto policy and an excess claim right exists against the negligent party's liability carrier, check the no-fault release carefully to be sure *only* your own company has been released and not any other.

Step-By-Step Recap

You will get the best results by carefully reading the materials and approaching the claim process in the order presented here. Starting out the process in an organized way will keep you organized throughout. A clear and well put together claim presented to an insurance adjuster who has no familiarity with your accident, injury, or damages will be financially more productive than one that is made in a sloppy or haphazard manner.

STEPS	MATERIALS TO USE	PURPOSE
STEP ONE Notify your liability carrier of motor vehicle accident.	Form No. 1	To notify your company when the accident causes property damage to your motor vehicle or bodily injury to you or any of your passengers while in your *motor vehicle* and to ensure coverage for you.
STEP TWO Notify the negligent party's insurance carrier (or your own) of intention to make a claim.	Form No. 2	To request name of negligent party's insurance carrier in any type of accident.
	Form No. 3	To notify negligent party's insurance carrier of an accident claim.
	Form No. 4	To notify your carrier of an uninsured motorist claim.
	Form No. 5	To notify your own insurance company of a no-fault auto claim.
	Form No. 6	For requesting insurance coverage information from the Secretary of State.
STEP THREE Gather the facts.	Written or recorded account of accident	To record personal, detailed account of facts prior to, during, and immediately after occurrence.
	Recorded description of bodily injuries	To record detailed account of personal injuries.
	Recorded description of property damage	To record detailed account of property damage.

STEPS	MATERIALS TO USE	PURPOSE
STEP THREE (Continued)	Photographs	To record the details of the accident scene, bodily injuries, and property damage.
	Diagram	To illustrate the location of accident.
	Form No. 7	To obtain police report.
	Form No. 8	To request witness to give a written statement.
	Form No. 9	To record witness' observation of an auto accident.
	Form No. 10	To record witness' observation of a pedestrian accident.
	Form No. 11	To record witness' observations of a slip and fall accident.
	Form No. 12	To record witness' observations of a property damage accident.
	Form No. 13	Request for uninsured motorist statement.
	Form No. 14	To prove the other driver had no insurance.
STEP FOUR Gather information for money damages.	Form No. 15	To request a medical report.
	Form No. 16	To enable treating doctors to verify your injuries on a standard medical report form.
	Form No. 17	To request your hospital or emergency room records.
	Form No. 18	To request lost time and wage verification.
	Form No. 19	To verify your time and wages lost.
	Form No. 20	To substantiate your time and/or income lost.
STEP FIVE Send information to the liability carrier.	Form No. 21	To inform negligent party's insurance company of supporting investigation.

STEPS	MATERIALS TO USE	PURPOSE
STEP FIVE (Continued)	Form No. 22	To send all items of damage to negligent party's carrier.
	Form No. 23	To send all items of damage to your own carrier for uninsured motorist claim.
	Form No. 24	To send medical bills for medical payment reimbursement.
	Form No. 25	To send all items of damages to own no-fault carrier.
STEP SIX Settle the claim with the insurance company.		Guidelines for negotiated settlements.
		Guidelines for reimbursed settlements.
		How to negotiate.
		Settling a reimbursement claim.
		Giving a statement.
		Signing releases.

The Million Dollar Case

When bodily injuries are serious or disabling, the financial recovery can surpass a million dollars. Seven figure compensation comes when the suffered injuries require a lifetime of medical care, deprive you of your ability to earn a living, or leave you severely handicapped or disfigured. Sometimes, destruction of valuable property along with infliction of bodily injury can warrant a super dollar insurance award.

It doesn't matter whether the injuries or damages resulted from a professional person's negligence, a defective product, a careless landlord, an inattentive driver, or a neglectful business owner. For purposes of compensation, the havoc caused by the accident can be repaid in multiples by the liability carrier.

Million Dollar Problems

Seeking compensation for serious injuries at the million dollar level is not a do-it-yourself project. Too many technical problems and too many legal nuances must be recognized and resolved. Several different persons, businesses, or property owners may be equally responsible for the accident. Each may pass the buck to the other in order to avoid payment. Pinning down the often subtle malpractice of an accountant, lawyer, or doctor can be difficult and frustrating. And the product defect that set into motion an unfortunate chain of events may require evaluation by a hard-to-find expert before any claim can be substantiated. In addition, proving that a specific injury justifies a seven figure recovery involves amassing from actuaries or economists precise financial data that projects the future dollar value of the claimant's life, work, and medical care expectancies.

An injury lawyer must labor at length to prepare a high valued claim just for settlement consideration. Almost as much work goes into the settlement presentation as would go into the trial itself. Your injury lawyer will provide expansive information accompanied by detailed evaluations and clarifying graphics. This helps the insurance company interpret each aspect of fault and injury. This artfully drawn proposal is organized in a way that will induce settlement. It can fetch for the injured client the most money possible.

Million Dollar Injuries

Imagine, if you will, the combination of expertise and preparation that was required in each of the following instances. Notice that the harm produced by the negligence was, almost without exception, devastating. It permanently altered every aspect of the affected life. Starting with the malpractice of professionals, the first case illustrates an injury resulting from misdiagnosis by a physician treating a patient.

A thirty-eight year old man was misdiagnosed by his doctor as having a brain tumor. The patient had an aneurysm. Before the surgery could be performed on the tumor, the aneurysm ruptured. The man suffered permanent paralysis on his entire right side as a result of the doctor's misdiagnosis.

In the next case, the failure of the physician to render proper treatment of an obvious condition caused the injury.

A forty-six year old man had suffered lacerations in an auto crash. The treating doctor at the hospital failed to immunize him against tetanus. The man was left with permanent brain damage from tetanus infection.

Damages awarded in medical malpractice cases may not always be given just for pain and suffering. Sometimes they include the expenses that flow as a natural result of the professional's negligence.

A healthy fifth child was born to a woman who had previously undergone a tubal ligation (a sterility procedure). She received compensation, not only for the pain and suffering and medical expenses connected with the child's birth, but was also given the anticipated costs of raising a child for eighteen years.

Lawyers, too, make mistakes. Here a client relied on the lawyer to take some action on his behalf. The lawyer was found negligent because he did not take action when he was professionally obligated to do so.

A man who had suffered brain damage, leaving him unable to speak, read or write because of the alleged malpractice of a doctor, sought legal advice on filing a claim. The lawyer offered to check the problem with a medical expert, although he did not believe the man had a viable claim. He told the client he would have the case evaluated and then inform the client if there was a good claim. The lawyer never did have the case evaluated. He allowed the statute of limitations to run out, barring forever the man's right to file the medical malpractice claim.

Sometimes the negligence of a professional, when combined with the use of a defective product, will bring forth tragic results. When this occurs, both the professional and the product manufacturer can be held responsible.

An eighteen-year-old girl, running a high fever, was admitted to a hospital. She was treated with a cooling blanket intended to reduce her fever. The blanket lacked automatic shut-off devices and omitted warnings against prolonged use. It cooled her hands and feet to the point of frostbite. Infection set in requiring amputation of both legs.

When the injury is caused by a defective product, any number of people in the distribution chain may be responsible for the defect. All those involved in the product's manufacture, assembly, distribution, or sale may be held accountable.

During a national gymnastic competition one of the star contestants was performing on the parallel bars. A mechanism used to lock one of the bars in place failed, allowing the bar to drop. The athlete fell on his head, sustaining permanent brain damage. Everyone from the manufacturer and distributor of the apparatus and the lock, to the owner of the stadium and promoter of the event, had potential liability for the injury.

Multiple liability regarding a defectively designed football helmet was also found in the following instance against a manufacturer, school district, and the high school football coaches.

During blocking and tackling practice, a student wearing the defectively designed helmet suffered a broken vertebrae, resulting in quadriplegia. The helmet failed to protect the neck area against great force that was used when certain blocking and tackling techniques were taught and practiced.

The owner of a product who allows people to use it without warning them of its inherent dangers can be held responsible along with the manufacturer *and* the person who readies the product for consumer use.

Above ground pool owners allowed neighborhood children to swim even when they weren't at home. The pool had no water depth markings, no warnings against diving, and its lining was not impact resistent. One visiting child dove into the pool striking her head on the bottom, causing quadriplegia. The homeowner, manufacturer, and installer were all held responsible.

Frequently, in the course of trying to collect for serious injuries, a controversial legal question will arise, requiring an additional lawsuit just to decide this question. It is only after the first problem is resolved that the injury case can be concluded.

A mother and daughter crossing a shopping center parking lot were struck by a car, pushing them into a building. Each lost a leg immediately upon impact. The auto was driven by an unlicensed woman being taught to drive by her husband. The husband's insurance policy excluded liability coverage for an unlicensed driver, but included coverage for anyone driving with the insured's permission. These two conflicting policy provisions were eventually interpreted as giving the husband coverage and thereby providing the injured women with compensation.

Property owners are sometimes careless too, creating disasters not only for their tenants but also for the casual passerby.

A bicyclist suffered severe vision loss when he fell off his bike on a city sidewalk in front of a condominium building. A drainage problem dating back to when the building was constructed caused a sidewalk slab to tilt. The property owner, not the city, was held accountable since he had never remedied the problem.

Consider next, the extent of the landlord's responsibility for the security of tenants.

A tenant was shot during a robbery attempt in the lobby of his building at 3:00 a.m. on a Sunday. The shooting left him wheelchair bound for life. The landlord was held responsible, partly because the part-time security guard he had hired was off duty at the time and partly because police records showed 80 reported criminal attacks at the building during the prior three years.

On occasion, property damage, when complicated by severe bodily injuries, will bring a million dollar recovery.

A couple bought a frame house for $110,000. It was warranted by the seller, after a professional inspection, to be free of termites. Within two years, the entire structure collapsed while the couple was sleeping. The home was destroyed, their personal property turned into debris, and both suffered serious bodily injuries in the collapse. The seller and the termite inspector were found jointly guilty, the seller for breach of warranty, and the inspector for negligence.

Each of these unfortunate instances drew over a million dollars in damages. Each required the prior evaluation of an expert in medicine, law, engineering, physics, construction, security, or entomology before a claim for negligence could be made. Each also required the application of sophisticated economic calculations and projections pertaining to life, work, and medical care expectancies before the amount of damages could be computed.

Keep in mind too, that each extraordinary claim generated a thorough investigation by the opposing insurance company. Experts were specifically hired to assess responsibility in a light that favored, not the injured person, but the insured. Company attorneys penetrated and turned around every fact looking for ways to minimize the dollar value of serious injuries. Should you ever seek a large recovery, your case would be subjected to the same intense scrutiny.

Preparing for the Million Dollar Battle

When misfortune of this magnitude strikes you or a loved one, you'll probably need a lawyer. It makes sense to fight strength with strength. It's one thing for an insurance company to pay, without resistance, $2,000, $5,000, or even $10,000. It's another matter when injury payment of $1,000,000, or more, is demanded from liability carriers. When that happens, they will use all available means to thwart a huge payment. They will contend their insured isn't responsible or that the claimant isn't seriously injured. They will argue over the smallest issues and litigate obscure technicalities for an eternity. The extensive fees generated by all this legal pandemonium (and insurance company lawyers are paid by the hour) don't amount to much when compared to the company's potential million dollar or more payout.

Your advocate in these instances should be a well-trained lawyer in the personal injury field . . . an attorney who ties his or her own financial rewards to the accurate analysis and forceful promotion of your case.

In most states, lawyers, except for admiralty and patent practitioners, are not allowed to hold themselves out as specialists in any one field of law. You'll probably want a lawyer who has, by design, a practice limited to personal injury.

Names of these attorneys can be learned from friends, neighbors, co-workers, business associates, or non-lawyer professionals, such as accountants or social workers. Find out the attorney's reputation by asking others who may have used his or her services. Compare the legal services you need with those previously furnished by this lawyer to your source. The lawyer may be fine for corporate or criminal defense work, but does this attorney routinely deal in personal injury cases?

If you get no leads from people you know, contact law school clinics in your area, local bar associations, non-legal self-help groups, phone directories that list lawyers by the types of law practiced, and even media advertisements. Any of these groups will supply you with a wealth of lawyers to contact. Your family lawyer or a professor at a nearby law school can also recommend an experienced personal injury attorney.

Explore and follow through all possibilities. Gather the names of two or three of the most qualified attorneys and then visit each one. Call first to set up an appointment. Most do not charge for a consultation, but check this when you call. Bring identical information to each interview. Ask the same kinds of questions, including any you may have about the fee arrangements, at each interview session. You can then make a fair comparison between lawyers.

Among the questions you'll need to ask:

- How much of your practice is devoted to representing injury claimants?
- How long have you been engaged in this type of practice?
- Do most of your cases settle or do you generally go to trial?
- Have you ever dealt with this insurance company before? If so, what can I expect from them?
- Will you be handling the case or will it be given to one of your associates?
- Have you ever represented a client who has the same type of injury as I have?
- What is the approximate dollar value of my case?
- How often can I expect communication from you regarding the status of my case?
- How long will it take before my case is over?
- What are your usual fee arrangements for handling this type of case and are these arrangements flexible?
- What kind of costs can I expect and how are they handled by your office?

- Will you and I have a written agreement regarding our fee and cost arrangements?

There are no right or wrong responses to these questions. The answers will simply make you aware of what you can expect and how your case will be handled.

The Legal Fee

Customarily, lawyers handle personal injury cases on a contingent fee basis. That is, the lawyer receives as a fee a percentage of the financial recovery won for you. No fee is earned if a recovery is not made. You are, however, always responsible for the court costs and investigative expenses advanced in pursuing your claim, whether it is ultimately won, lost, or settled.

A contingent fee works best with personal injury claims because most people cannot spend an average of $125 per hour for possibly 100 hours of legal time — and then lose the case, receiving no money at all. Moreover, human nature, being what it is, lawyers tend to put in more effort when they take the risk with you and work for a portion of your recovery.

You'll find different kinds of contingent fee arrangements, those fees based on a straight percentage of recovery and those fees based upon a graduated dollar amount of the recovery.

The lawyer's contingency fee is often negotiable, barring any special state laws setting this amount. The usual range is between 33⅓ percent and 40 percent. A lower percentage rate may be charged where the attorney is hired to collect from your own insurer either medical pay or no-fault benefits. A higher than 40 percent fee may be appropriate where the case is especially difficult, the problems are unusually complex, the legal issues novel, or a jury trial or an appeal is necessary.

Four different levels of contingent fees may be used in your agreement, depending upon the stage at which the claim or lawsuit ends:

1. When the case is settled without a lawsuit.
2. When the case is settled after a lawsuit is filed but before a trial begins.
3. When the case is tried to verdict.
4. When a judgment is given for a certain amount after an appeal.

At each stage the percentage of contingent fee may be increased.

In addition to this kind of arrangement, contingent fees can also be predicated upon the dollar amount of recovery. For example, the lawyer may charge 33⅓ percent of all sums up to $50,000, 25 percent of all sums between $50,000 and $150,000, and then 20 percent of all funds recovered over that amount. Depending on the expected size of the compensation, this approach may also be combined with the settlement/judgment stage option.

Cover All Bases – Then Decide

Pursue with the lawyer, as well, expected costs of your claim or lawsuit. Ordinarily these include investigative expenses, expert evaluations or witness' fees, subpoena fees, filing costs, deposition expenses, and other preparation costs. The lawyer should be able to approximate these for you. Some lawyers require a partial advance of costs before work is done on your case.

Feel free to question the attorney on any other matters you believe are important.

Finally, after reviewing all this information, size up this lawyer. What do your instincts tell you? Did the attorney evade your questions or answer them directly? Did he or she exhibit some flexibility with regard to the legal fee arrangements or were you given a "take it or leave it" situation? Did the attorney inform you of the cases's strengths and vulnerabilities or did the interview turn into a self-promotion session? Think it over. Be aware that you and this attorney may be working together for three or four years. Make your decision based upon the information you learned at the interview as processed through your own judgment.

Once you've made this decision, come to a fee agreement with the lawyer. Be sure these arrangements are made in writing and that you receive a signed copy of the agreement. Read it over making sure that it includes and accurately reflects the agreed to terms. Then sign it. One copy stays in the lawyers files, the other in your files. Now you're ready to work together to successfully conclude your claim.

The What-Not-To's and Why-Not-To's

Certain types of accidental injury claims cannot be processed with this self-help format. The information and ready-to-use forms in this book are not meant to be used for the special kinds of accidents explained here. Should you ever have an injury claim that falls into one of these categories, consult a lawyer.

Dramshop Claims

Many states have laws which allow a person who is physically injured by an intoxicated person or allow a person who is injured in their means of support as a result of someone else's intoxication, to make a claim for injury or loss of support against the business furnishing the liquor and the building owner where the liquor was sold. The laws creating *dramshop* rights for injuries or loss of support differ from state to state and are replete with technical requirements, damage recovery limits and time limits for filing a lawsuit. A few examples:

> While in a restaurant where liquor is sold, another patron becomes intoxicated and shoots a gun, causing you injury. You have a claim against the restaurant and building owner, if your state has such a dramshop law. In addition, you may have a negligence claim against the restaurant.

> You were injured and unable to work for six months as a result of an automobile accident that occurred while you were driving under the influence of alcohol. Your spouse may have a dramshop claim for loss of support against the bar and the owner of the building where you became intoxicated.

Death Claims by Surviving Family

Each state has its own laws monitoring financial recoveries when an accidental injury results in the death of a family member. The laws on who has the right to make a claim and for what kinds of damages vary from state to state. In addition, a probate estate must be opened and an administrator appointed.

Injuries on the Job

Specific laws in almost all states create unique claim rights for employees accidentally injured while at work. The method of making a claim, the types of damages recoverable, and widely differing interpretations of what "while at work" means, foreclose the use of this self-help format for this type of claim.

Underinsured Motorist Claim

At times, a negligent driver will have some liability coverage, but not enough to compensate you for injuries caused by the accident. If, in your state, you are able to purchase underinsured motorist insurance coverage and it is in an amount greater than the negligent driver's liability coverage, an additional injury claim can be made with your own carrier after exhaustion of the negligent driver's liability insurance benefits. This is a complex area requiring interpretation of insurance contracts. Here's how it could work:

> As a result of a motor vehicle accident, your injury claim is valued at $20,000. The negligent driver has liability insurance coverage only in the sum of $15,000. You have purchased underinsured motorist coverage in the amount of $30,000. You can collect $5,000 from your insurance company.

Claims Against Public Entities or Government

Where the person responsible for your property damage or injury is a public entity or government unit, such as a state, county, city, village, housing authority, transit authority, school district, park district, or an agency of the federal government, shortened time periods for filing claims and notice requirements are set by law. If these special rules are not strictly followed, your right to a claim is lost. Examples of cases that should be given special attention:

> You fell and were injured when you tripped over a mail cart that was rolling toward you while you were mailing a package at the post office (agency of the federal government).

> Your child was burned while cooking in a home economics class (school district).

> You slipped on a wet floor while visiting a patient at a county hospital causing you injury (local government unit).

Intentional Injuries or Damage

If a person intentionally throws a brick through your office window or swings at you and breaks your nose after a minor traffic accident, legal remedies are available. Usually though, insurance does not cover these intentional acts.

Claims Against Professionals and Health Providers

Injuries sometimes result from the negligence of professionals such as doctors, dentists, lawyers, engineers, architects, or therapists, and health providers such as hospitals, medical or dental groups, or clinics. State laws vary on the time limitations for making such a claim. Evaluation of the alleged negligence by experts in the field must be made before a claim can be successful.

Injuries Caused by a Defective Product

If you are injured when using a product that is defective either because it is not labeled properly or because of some actual product malfunction or defect, self-help procedures usually will not be effective in gaining a recovery. Where there are problems in proving the existence of a defect as in the *second* example below, or when the injury is serious as in the *third* example below, don't jeopardize the claim by trying to process it yourself. However, in simpler cases, as in the *first* example below, self help may be the method to use.

You break a tooth on a piece of metal inside a Rooty Tooty cupcake you purchased at the local chain store. Pursue your claim against both the Rooty Tooty company and the chain store that sold the goods.

Your child's arm is smashed causing broken bones when an automatic car window fails to respond to the release button; this defect is difficult to prove and a lawyer is necessary.

Your child fell down on cement and broke bones in his arm when a wheel broke off his roller skates the first time he used them. Negligence in this situation could be technically difficult to prove.

The When-To's

It is only fair that the person or business that has caused you injury or damage know at some point in time whether or not you are going to bring a lawsuit against them. That is why every state has created time limits called *statutes of limitation* that tell you how long you have after a certain kind of occurrence to file a lawsuit against the other person or business. If you don't bring a lawsuit within this time period, you lose forever your right to do so. Your claim is lost or abandoned. The people responsible for the accident are never again put in jeopardy of financial exposure for your claim. The courts strictly enforce statute of limitation rules.

Time Limits

No universal statute of limitation rules are in use across the fifty states. One state may have a one year time limit on the filing of bodily injury claims, while a second state will extend this period to two or three years. And within one single state, there may be two different time limits for the filing of bodily injury and property damage claims.

When using this self-help format, if you cannot settle your claim within ten months of the accident, contact your public library information service or an attorney to find out your state's time limit for filing lawsuits for your type of injury or damage. The time limit for filing a lawsuit against your own company may be different than that for filing the same type of lawsuit against another person.

If no settlement is in sight after the ten month period either because you've been unable to gather all the necessary information or the insurance company is uncooperative, contact a lawyer. If you wish to pursue your claim, an attorney can file a lawsuit for you within the prescribed time limits.

A Few Other Cautions to Keep in Mind

You cannot, where you have made an uninsured motorist claim, accept money from or sign a release with the uninsured motorist. This will violate the provisions of your insurance policy and may lead to a denial of your uninsured motorist benefits.

Where you've collected medical payments under your own policy, your insurance carrier may have the right to reimbursement for these if you should collect personal injury damages from the negligent party's insurance company.

Conclusion

This book has tried to expand your world by imparting clear, practical, and readily usable information. This information was once the exclusive property of lawyers. It now belongs to you as well.

You now possess skills and techniques from which you can reap success—over and over again—for both injury claims and property damage mishaps. No longer will you need to feel totally reliant on a lawyer. This self-help format, combined with your initiative and perserverance, can help you collect *money damages* for yourself. No unnecessary legal fees, no added costs. You keep it all.

But you can't have that success, that freedom from lawyers and legal fees, unless you give it a try.

Any awkwardness or reluctance you may have will vanish once you get started. It's easier than you think to collect damage information or negotiate the claim's value with an insurance company. And when the settlement process comes to a satisfying conclusion, you may surprise yourself. But you won't surprise us.

Appendix A
What You Should Know About No-Fault Insurance

The nation is almost evenly divided between fault and no-fault systems of insurance. Some no-fault states make purchase of these benefits optional. Others make this type of auto insurance coverage mandatory for all drivers.

Various types of no-fault insurance laws exist. Most restrict, in some manner, one's right to file a claim or lawsuit against the responsible person after no-fault benefits have been used. A few allow claims and lawsuits without limitation even before all no-fault benefits have been exhausted. These apply when certain kinds of injuries have been sustained. A small number allow claims or lawsuits without limitation. (For workings of the various no-fault systems see Step Six of this book.) Fault states always allow claims and lawsuits against the negligent party without restrictions.

Laws frequently are changed by state legislatures. A fault state today could be a no-fault state within the next six months or vice versa. Always contact your state Department of Insurance to learn the most up-to-date laws. (See Appendix B for the addresses and phone numbers of your state's Department of Insurance.) Current information pertaining to each state's fault or no-fault laws is set out in the following *Auto Liability and No-Fault Chart.* It tells you what you can expect from your state's insurance laws.

STATE AUTO LIABILITY & NO-FAULT LAWS

STATE	TYPE OF STATE fault or no-fault	NO-FAULT BENEFITS	WHEN A CLAIM OR LAWSUIT CAN BE FILED AGAINST RESPONSIBLE PERSON'S INSURANCE COMPANY
Alabama	Fault		Anytime
Alaska	Fault		Anytime
Arizona	Fault		Anytime
Arkansas	Optional No-Fault	Medical and Hospital $2,000 Wage Loss—70% up to 140 per week (8-days waiting period, maximum 52 weeks) Death—$5,000	
California	Fault		Anytime
Colorado	Mandatory No-Fault	Medical Expense—$25,000 Rehabilitation—$25,000 Loss of Income up to $125 per week per week for 52 weeks Death—$1,000	After general damages exceed $500 for medical and rehabilitation expenses OR Permanent disfigurement Permanent disability Dismemberment Loss of earnings for more than 52 weeks Death
Connecticut	Mandatory No-Fault	Medical, Hospital and Funeral—$2,000 Limit Lost Wages, survivors' loss, and substitute service—$5,000 Wage loss up to $200 per week Substitute service and survivors— 85% of actual loss	After general damages exceed $400 for medical bills OR Where permanent injury, bone fracture, disfigurement, dismemberment, or death

STATE AUTO LIABILITY & NO-FAULT LAWS (Continued)

STATE	TYPE OF STATE fault or no-fault	NO-FAULT BENEFITS	WHEN A CLAIM OR LAWSUIT CAN BE FILED AGAINST RESPONSIBLE PERSON'S INSURANCE COMPANY
Delaware	Optional No-Fault	$10,000 per person $20,000 per accident These figures include medical, loss of income, loss of services and funeral ($2,000 limit)	Anytime – however, benefits received cannot be used as evidence in suits for general damages
District of Columbia	Fault		Anytime
Florida	Mandatory No-Fault	80% of medical expenses 60% of wage loss Death – $1,750 Benefits not to exceed $10,000 total	If the injury results in death, permanent disfigurement, or disability or dismemberment
Georgia	Mandatory No-Fault	Medical Expenses – $2,500 per person Wage Loss- 85% up to $200 per week up to $2,500 Death – $1,500 Benefits not to exceed $5,000 total	After general damages exceed $500 for medical expenses OR Death, fractured bone, permanent disfigurement, dismemberment, permanent loss (partial or total) of sight or hearing, or disability for ten consecutive days
Hawaii	Mandatory No-Fault	Medical Expenses – $15,000 Wage Loss – 100% up to $800 per month Death – $1,500 Benefits not to exceed $15,000 total	After general damages exceed $5,200 for medical expenses OR If injury results in death, significant permanent loss of use of a part or function of the body, or serious disfigurement which causes mental or emotional suffering

STATE AUTO LIABILITY & NO-FAULT LAWS (Continued)

STATE	TYPE OF STATE fault or no-fault	NO-FAULT BENEFITS	WHEN A CLAIM OR LAWSUIT CAN BE FILED AGAINST RESPONSIBLE PERSON'S INSURANCE COMPANY
Idaho	Fault		Anytime
Illinois	Fault		Anytime
Indiana	Fault		Anytime
Iowa	Fault		Anytime
Kansas	Mandatory No-Fault	Medical – $2,000 Wage Loss up to $650 per month Rehabilitation – $2,000 Substitute service – $12 per day (maximum 365 days) Funeral – $1,000	After general damages exceed $500 for medical costs OR If the injury results in permanent disfigurement, fracture of a weight-bearing bone; a compound, comminuted, displaced, or compressed fracture; loss of body member; permanent loss of a body function; or death
Kentucky	Optional No-Fault	Medical Expenses – $10,000 Wage Loss – 85% up to $200 per week Death – $1,000 Benefits not to exceed $10,000 total	After general damages exceed $1,000 for non-economical loss OR If the injury results in death; permanent disfigurement; a fracture to a weight-bearing bone; a compound, comminuted, displaced, or compressed fracture; loss of body member; permanent injury or permanent loss of a bodily function
Louisiana	Fault		Anytime

STATE AUTO LIABILITY & NO-FAULT LAWS (Continued)

STATE	TYPE OF STATE fault or no-fault	NO-FAULT BENEFITS	WHEN A CLAIM OR LAWSUIT CAN BE FILED AGAINST RESPONSIBLE PERSON'S INSURANCE COMPANY
Maine	Fault		Anytime
Maryland	Mandatory No-Fault	Medical, hospital, funeral, wage loss, and substitute service expenses – $2,500	Anytime
Massachusetts	Mandatory No-Fault	Medical, funeral, wage loss, and substitute service up to – $2,000 Wage Loss limited to 75% of actual loss	After general damages exceed $500 for medical expenses OR If the injury results in death; loss of all or part of body member, permanent and serious disfigurement, loss of sight, hearing, or a fracture
Michigan	Mandatory No-Fault	Medical and hospital – Unlimited Funeral up to $1,000 Wage Loss – $2,049 per month for a maximum of 36 months Substitute service – $20 per day payable to victim or survivor	If injury results in death, serious impairment of body function, or permanent serious disfigurement
Minnesota	Mandatory No-Fault	Medical – $20,000 Wage Loss – $10,000	After general damages exceed $2,000 for medical expenses
Mississippi	Fault		Anytime
Missouri	Fault		Anytime
Montana	Fault		Anytime
Nebraska	Fault		Anytime

STATE AUTO LIABILITY & NO-FAULT LAWS (Continued)

STATE	TYPE OF STATE fault or no-fault	NO-FAULT BENEFITS	WHEN A CLAIM OR LAWSUIT CAN BE FILED AGAINST RESPONSIBLE PERSON'S INSURANCE COMPANY
Nevada	Fault		Anytime
New Hampshire	Fault		Anytime
New Jersey	Mandatory No-Fault	Medical and Hospital – Unlimited Wage Loss – $100 per week for one year Substitute services – up to $12 per day and $4,380 per person Funeral – $1,000 Survivors' benefit equal to amount to be received had victim lived	After general damages exceed $200 for medical expenses less hospital AND Cannot recover if injuries are confined to soft tissue
New Mexico	Fault		Anytime
New York	Mandatory No-Fault	Reasonable and necessary medical and rehabilitation expenses Wage Loss up to 80% of lost earnings, Maximum $1,000 per month for three years Substitute service – $25 per day up to one year Benefits not to exceed $50,000 per person	If economic losses are in excess of $50,000 OR If the injury results in death; dismemberment, disfigurement, fracture, permanent consequential limitation of use of body organ, or significant limitation of a body function
North Carolina	Fault		Anytime

STATE AUTO LIABILITY & NO-FAULT LAWS (Continued)

STATE	TYPE OF STATE fault or no-fault	NO-FAULT BENEFITS	WHEN A CLAIM OR LAWSUIT CAN BE FILED AGAINST RESPONSIBLE PERSON'S INSURANCE COMPANY
North Dakota	Mandatory No-Fault	Medical Expenses – $15,000 Wage Loss – 85% up to $150 per week Death – $1,000 Benefits not to exceed $15,000 total	After general damages exceed $1,000 for medical expenses OR If the injury results in death; dismemberment; serious and permanent disfigurement, or disability for 60 days
Ohio	Fault		Anytime
Oklahoma	Fault		Anytime
Oregon	Mandatory No-Fault	Medical – $5,000 Wage Loss – 70% up to $750 per month for a maximum of 52 weeks Loss of services – $18 per day (14-day retroactive waiting period and maximum 52 weeks)	Anytime
Pennsylvania	Fault		Anytime
Rhode Island	Fault		Anytime
South Carolina	Optional No-Fault	Medical – $1,000 Wage Loss – 100% up to three years	Anytime
South Dakota	Optional No-Fault	Medical – $2,000 Wage Loss – $60 per week (14-day waiting period, 52 week maximum) Death – $10,000	Anytime

STATE AUTO LIABILITY & NO-FAULT LAWS (Continued)

STATE	TYPE OF STATE fault or no-fault	NO-FAULT BENEFITS	WHEN A CLAIM OR LAWSUIT CAN BE FILED AGAINST RESPONSIBLE PERSON'S INSURANCE COMPANY
Tennessee	Fault		Anytime
Texas	Optional No-Fault	Medical, funeral, wage loss, loss services – $2,500	Anytime
Utah	Mandatory No-Fault	Medical and Hospital – $2,000 Wage Loss – 85% of gross income up to $150 per week for 52 weeks Substitute service – $12 per day, maximum 365 days Funeral – $1,000 Survivors – $2,000 (3-day waiting period for wage and service loss where total disability is less than two weeks)	After general damages exceed $500 for medical expenses OR If the injury results in permanent disfigurement, fracture, dismemberment, permanent disability, or death
Vermont	Fault		Anytime
Virginia	Fault		Anytime
Washington	Fault		Anytime
West Virginia	Fault		Anytime
Wisconsin	Fault		Anytime
Wyoming	Fault		Anytime

84

Appendix B
These State Agencies Can Help

The property and casualty insurance business is regulated in each state by insurance commissions or departments of insurance. These all have a consumer services section equipped to review consumer complaints against insurance companies.

These agencies cannot place a value on property damage or bodily injury claims. They can, however, intercede on the consumer's behalf when a particular insurance company fails to pay a claim or does not deal with the claimant in a timely or businesslike manner. They also can act on the consumer's behalf to get a claim paid, but only where the insurance company's responsibility for a specified amount has already been established and the claim is due.

These agencies also furnish information to the public regarding the number of consumer complaints received against each insurance company doing business within the state's borders. They can also tell you if you live in a fault or no-fault insurance state. In case you need their help, the addresses and phone numbers for each follow.

STATE INSURANCE COMMISSIONS

ALABAMA
Commissioner of Insurance
135 South Union Street
Montgomery, AL 36130-3401
(205) 269-3550

ALASKA
Director of Insurance
Pouch "D"
Juneau, AK 99811
(907) 465-2515

ARIZONA
Director of Insurance
1601 West Jefferson
Phoenix, AZ 85007
(602) 255-4862

ARKANSAS
Insurance Commissioner
400 University Tower Building
Little Rock, AR 72204
(501) 371-1325

CALIFORNIA
Insurance Commissioner
600 South Commonwealth—14th Floor
Los Angeles, CA 90005
(213) 736-2551

COLORADO
Commissioner of Insurance
303 West Colfax Avenue—5th Floor
Denver, CO 80204
(303) 534-8871

CONNECTICUT
Insurance Commissioner
State Office Building
165 Capitol Avenue
Hartford, CT 06106
(203) 566-5275

DELAWARE
Insurance Commissioner
21 The Green
Dover, DE 19901
(302) 736-4251

DISTRICT OF COLUMBIA
Superintendent of Insurance
614 H Street, N.W., Suite 512
Washington, DC 20001
(202) 727-7421

FLORIDA
Insurance Commissioner
State Capitol
Plaza Level 11
Tallahassee, FL 32301
(904) 488-3440

GEORGIA
Insurance Commissioner
Floyd Memorial Building
200 Piedmont Avenue, S.E.
West Tower—7th Floor
Atlanta, GA 30334
(404)656-2056

HAWAII
Insurance Commissioner
P.O. Box 3614
Honolulu, HI 96811
(808)548-5450

IDAHO
Director of Insurance
700 West State Street
Boise, ID 83720
(208)334-2250

ILLINOIS
Director of Insurance
320 West Washington St—4th Floor
Springfield, IL 62767
(217)782-4515

INDIANA
Commissioner of Insurance
509 State Office Building
Indianapolis, IN 46204
(317)232-2386

IOWA
Commissioner of Insurance
State Office Building
G23 Ground Floor
Des Moines, IA 50319
(515)281-5705

KANSAS
Commissioner of Insurance
420 South West Ninth Street
Topeka, KS 66612
(913)296-3071

KENTUCKY
Insurance Commissioner
151 Elkhorn Court
Frankfort, KY 40601
(502)564-3630

LOUISIANA
Commissioner of Insurance
950 North 5th Street
Baton Rouge, LA 70801
(504)342-5328

MAINE
Superintendent of Insurance
State Office Building
State House, Station 34
Augusta, ME 04333
(207)289-3101

MARYLAND
Insurance Commissioner
501 St. Paul Place—7th Floor South
Baltimore, MD 21202
(301)659-4027

MASSACHUSETTS
Commissioner of Insurance
100 Cambridge Street
Boston MA 02202
(617)727-3333

MICHIGAN
Insurance Commissioner
P.O. Box 30220
611 West Ottawa Street
Lansing, MI 48933
(517)373-9273

MINNESOTA
Commissioner of Commerce
500 Metro Square Building
St. Paul, MN 55101
(612)296-6907

MISSISSIPPI
Commissioner of Insurance
1804 Walter Sillers Building
P.O. Box 79
Jackson, MS 39205
(601)359-3569

MISSOURI
Director of Insurance
301 West High Street 6 North
P.O. Box 690
Jefferson City, MO 65102
(314)751-2451

MONTANA
Commissioner of Insurance
Mitchell Building
P.O. Box 4009
Helena, MT 59601
(406) 444-2996

NEBRASKA
Director of Insurance
301 Centennial Mall, South
P.O. Box 94699
Lincoln, NE 68509
(402) 471-2201-Ext. 238

NEVADA
Commissioner of Insurance
Nye Building
201 South Fall Street
Carson City, NV 89710
(702) 885-4270

NEW HAMPSHIRE
Insurance Commissioner
169 Manchester Street
Concord, NH 03301
(603) 271-2261

NEW JERSEY
Commissioner of Insurance
201 East State Street
Trenton, NJ 08625
(609) 292-5363

NEW MEXICO
Superintendent of Insurance
PERA Building
P.O. Drawer 1269
Santa Fe, NM 87501
(505) 827-4535

NEW YORK
Superintendent of Insurance
160 West Broadway
New York, NY 10013
(213) 602-0429

NORTH CAROLINA
Commissioner of Insurance
Dobbs Building
P.O. Box 26387
Raleigh, NC 27611
(919) 733-7343

NORTH DAKOTA
Commissioner of Insurance
Capitol Building—Fifth Floor
Bismarck, ND 58505
(701) 224-2444

OHIO
Director of Insurance
2100 Stella Court
Columbus, OH 43215
(614) 466-3584

OKLAHOMA
Insurance Commissioner
408 Will Rogers Memorial Building
Oklahoma City, OK 73105
(405) 521-2828

OREGON
Insurance Commissioner
158 12th Street, N.E.
Salem, OR 97310
(503) 378-4271

PENNSYLVANIA
Insurance Commissioner
Strawberry Square—13th Floor
Harrisburg, PA 17120
(717) 787-5173

RHODE ISLAND
Insurance Commissioner
100 North Main Street
Providence, RI 02903
(401) 277-2223

SOUTH CAROLINA
Chief Insurance Commissioner
2711 Middleburg Drive
P.O. Box 4067
Columbia, SC 29204
(803) 758-3266

SOUTH DAKOTA
Director of Insurance
Insurance Building
320 North Nicollet
Pierre, SD 57501
(605) 773-3563

TENNESSEE
Commissioner of Insurance
114 State Office Building
Nashville, TN 37219
(615) 741-2241

TEXAS
Commissioner of Insurance
11110 San Jacinto Boulevard
Austin, TX 78786
(512) 475-2273

UTAH
Commissioner of Insurance
160 East 300 South
P.O. Box 5803
Salt Lake City, UT 84110
(801) 530-6400

VERMONT
Commissioner of Insurance
State Office Building
120 State Street
Montpelier, VT 05602
(802) 828-3301

VIRGINIA
Commissioner of Insurance
700 Jefferson Building
P.O. Box 1157
Richmond, VA 28209
(804) 786-3741

WASHINGTON
Insurance Commissioner
Insurance Building AQ21
Olympia, WA 98504
(206) 753-7301

WEST VIRGINIA
Insurance Commissioner
2100 Washington Street, East
Charleston, WV 25305
(304) 348-3386

WISCONSIN
Commissioner of Insurance
P.O. Box 7873
123 West Washington Avenue
Madison, WI 53707
(608) 266-0102

WYOMING
Insurance Commissioner
2424 Pioneer Avenue
Cheyenne, WY 82002
(307) 777-7401

Disclaimer

Settle It Yourself gives you the basic procedures for making accidental injury and property damage claims against an insurance company. The forms and techniques published here for consumer use are those routinely used by lawyers representing clients in similar situations.

However, the authors are not, by furnishing this information to you, acting as your attorneys or representing you in any way when making your claim. If questions do arise during the claim process that are not answered in this book, consult with an attorney who practices exclusively in this field before finalizing your settlement. Some questions you may want answered by a lawyer:

1. Is the settlement offer within the range of fairness?

2. How much time do I have before I must file a lawsuit or lose that right under the statute of limitations?

3. By signing the release for the liability carrier, am I giving up rights I don't know about?

Where serious injuries involving permanent disability occur – a fatality to someone in your family, loss of future earnings for a significant period of time, protracted medical care, or serious disfigurement – *always* consult with an attorney specializing in the personal injury field before settling your claim with the insurance company.

Severe injuries stemming from defective products or those caused by the action or inactions of professionals, such as doctors, hospitals, dentists, lawyers, accountants, or therapists, always need an attorney's evaluation. Proving that defects exist in a product (or in a product's labeling) or that a professional has been negligent, requires technical evaluation, which a lawyer must obtain and assess to promote your claim.